# Sermons on Suicide

# SERMONS ON SUICIDE

## James T. Clemons
### editor

Westminster/John Knox Press
Louisville, Kentucky

Scripture quotations from the Revised Standard Version of the Bible are copyrighted 1946, 1952, © 1971, 1973 by the Division of Christian Education of the National Council of the Churches of Christ in the U.S.A. and are used by permission.

Excerpts from *The New Jerusalem Bible* are copyright © 1985 by Darton, Longman & Todd, Ltd, and Doubleday, a division of Bantam Doubleday Dell Publishing Group, Inc. Reprinted by permission.

Sermon 11, "When Pain Is Too Much," by Paul E. Van Dine, was first published in Master Sermon Series, volume 17, number 10, and is reprinted by permission. Excerpts from *Cold Sassy Tree,* by Olive Ann Burns, are copyright © 1984 by Olive Ann Burns. Reprinted by permission of Ticknor & Fields/Clarion Books, a Houghton Mifflin Company.

Sermon 13, "Suicide: An Unpardonable Sin?" © 1983 by the author, Wasena F. Wright, Jr., under the title "Suicide and the Church."

Portions of sermon 8, "Is Suicide Ever a Christian's Right?" were previously published under the title "Christian Perspectives on Suicide" in *The Christian Century,* Oct. 30, 1985, and are used by permission.

Book design by Gene Harris

First edition

Published by Westminster/John Knox Press
Louisville, Kentucky

PRINTED IN THE UNITED STATES OF AMERICA

9  8  7  6  5  4  3  2  1

**Library of Congress Cataloging-in-Publication Data**

Sermons on suicide / James T. Clemons, editor. — 1st ed.
    p.   cm.
Bibliography: p.
ISBN 0-664-25071-8

   1. Suicide—Religious aspects—Christianity. 2. Suicide—Sermons. 3. Sermons, American. I. Clemons, James T.
HV6545.S337 1989                        88-35184
241'.697—dc19                              CIP

# Contents

# Preface

Over the past two decades, America has been stunned by shocking statistics and tragic accounts of suicide in almost every segment of our society. National, city, and regional newspapers, professional magazines and journals, and radio and television programs have repeatedly addressed one or more phases of this very complex, emotion-laden, and morally confusing subject.

In the midst of almost relentless media attention focused on a topic affecting millions of people, it is strange indeed that so little has been said about suicide from the pulpit. I have often put the question to lay people: "Have you ever heard a sermon on suicide?" And, to preachers: "Have you ever preached on the subject, apart from a funeral service?" Almost always, the answer has been a simple no. Occasionally a preacher has added reflectively, "But you know, I really should."

There are, of course, some obvious reasons for this reluctance: lack of biblical knowledge and ethical guidance, the long period in church history in which suicide in any form was damned, and the fear of inadvertently encouraging someone to commit suicide. But none of these factors, singly or together, can outweigh the responsibility of religious communities to provide that combination of thorough exegesis, prophetic urgency, and pastoral direction which can best be given from the pulpit. Without strong support from the preaching ministry, all other efforts by faithful individuals and communities are severely hampered.

The purpose of this book is to encourage preachers to address a subject that not only is of national concern but also affects a large percentage of their listening congregation. My underlying assumption is that the pulpit is still one of the most effective means of religious instruction, pastoral care, and social action. When preachers don't address significant issues in some way, regardless of how controversial or difficult they may be, one of two messages comes thundering through the silence: Either preachers don't care or they don't know what to say.

Certainly no one has forced preachers to ignore the issue, and I cannot believe my colleagues, so outspoken on a host of other difficult and controversial issues, are either unaware or uncaring. They know as well as anyone, and better than most, about the pain felt by persons who attempt suicide and by the friends and family members who survive the self-chosen deaths of fifty thousand Americans each year.

On the positive side, individual persons of faith are much involved in suicide research, prevention, and caregiving. An increasing number of churches and synagogues are initiating preventive programs and support groups. But outside of an occasional theological discussion, usually in obscure journals or heavy tomes, all too little is available to help religious communities to see the complexity of the issue, gain a proper perspective, and begin working through the ethical problems and social stigmas in order to make an intentional, informed, and faithful response.

If this larger, urgent need is to be met, pastors, rabbis, and others who speak to the church or synagogue must become more vocal. They must provide in the area of suicide, the kind of effective leadership they have traditionally given on important social issues in the past. Their sermons, as always, must be biblical, theological, and pastoral, informed by historical, sociological, medical, and psychological understanding.

This collection of sermons, crafted by preachers from both the parish and the theological community, is presented with the hope that it will encourage other preachers in all religious groups to fill a crucial need. It seeks to do this in two ways. First, it demonstrates that the subject of suicide, for all its complexity and all the negativism of past history, can be addressed in a positive, straightforward way. It affirms the listening congregation as those who can hear the matter presented in the context of both faith and the world's wisdom, and who can then be trusted to make a faithful, caring, and loving response.

Second, it provides a veritable feast of biblical texts and interpretations, statistics,[1] medical insights, personal illustrations, and practical suggestions on which preachers can rely while engaged in their homiletical tasks. The individual sermons were selected from many I have painstakingly gleaned from preachers across the country, representing a broad spectrum of religious and theological perspectives. In some cases, scripture quotations have been made inclusive.

Whether or not a larger number of sermons on suicide will be preached, I have no way of knowing, although two of the sermons in this collection came as a result of my specific request. That in itself is a tremendous encouragement to believe that, someday soon, religious communities across the country will be better prepared and more strongly motivated to address the many personal and social problems that suicide forces upon us.

---

[1] Because the writers of these sermons did their research at various times, using different sources, the statistics used in the sermons may not all be consistent. Therefore, the preacher who is developing a sermon on the theme will want to check current information.

# Sermons on Suicide

# Introduction

Throughout its long history, from Moses to the present moment, preaching has provided several basic functions for Jewish and Christian communities. It instructs the faithful in their origins and beliefs. It helps to translate faith into ethical decisions and behavior. It strengthens and encourages those who are struggling with personal tragedy or community distress. It urges and guides faithful hearers as they wrestle with the fundamental life-and-death issues that confront each generation. It points out their pestering weaknesses and condemns their unconscionable sins. At times, it issues strident calls for reforms in attitudes, institutions, and even governments that have become an abomination to decency, dignity, and freedom in society. No wonder that those who preach, even after forty years or more, can still find excitement and challenge in their task!

It is in this noble tradition that sermons on suicide are to be viewed. The subject has always been broad and deep. Saul, Samson, Socrates, Judas—some would even say Jesus —enter into the discussion, and even these few self-chosen deaths represent the heroic, altruistic, tragic, rational, and perhaps irrational dimensions in human experience.

Today, suicide remains a complex issue, made all the more urgent because it is so prevalent, painful, and costly. It is a subject which by its enormity demands the attention of religious communities, calling on them to reexamine their traditional attitudes and questioning their present responses. Accounts in the Bible and history, discussions in philosophy and theology, research in sociology and medicine, deliberations in ethics and jurisprudence, and innumerable artistic depictions in novels, poetry, plays, and opera are constant reminders that the subject is still very much with us, quite apart from current statistics and media attention.

All these factors, to which must be added the intense existential dimension, become avenues for the preacher in approaching the subject of suicide. At the same time, it is incumbent upon those called to preach a word in due season to see all the relevant issues from a proper, informed, and wholesome perspective. The examples in this collection represent several of these dimensions and make use of many of the avenues leading to a deeper understanding of the subject. By way of introduction, then, and to put them in their deserved historical framework, I shall comment briefly on the history of preaching on suicide and the ways in which Jewish and Christian communities have wrestled with suicide in terms of faith and action.

### Biblical References to Suicide

We begin with the reminder that the Bible is itself a form of preaching. Not only does it contain many "sermons" (those of Moses in Deuteronomy, of Amos, Isaiah, and Jeremiah, of Jesus, of the apostles in Acts, and of the seer in Revelation come quickly to mind), but, as holy scripture, the Bible stands as a proclamation of faith in written form. Thus, although none of the biblical writers announced their topic as suicide, their accounts of self-chosen or self-attempted death said something about the subject to those who accepted the texts as holy scripture.

It has often been pointed out that none of the biblical suicides were actually condemned. Samson prayed that he might have strength to avenge the Philistines who had captured and tormented him (Judg. 16:28–31). The Lord granted his request to die with them, and he was remembered, even in the book of Hebrews, as one of Israel's faithful heroes.

Saul's tragic life ended when, after facing defeat and capture and torture, he fell upon his own sword. He was followed in this act by his armor-bearer (1 Samuel 31). Abimelech, having been bashed on the head by a female defender of the city he was attacking, asked that his armor-bearer slay him. The reason he gave says more about the negative way women were thought of in his day than about the evils of suicide: "Take your sword and thrust me through, lest men say of me, 'A woman killed him'" (Judg. 9:50–54).

Ahithophel, having seen his advice to Absalom rejected for that of another confidant, "set his house in order" and hanged himself (2 Sam. 17:23). Zimri, facing capture as his opponents besieged his city, set fire to the house in which he was living and died in its flames (1 Kings 16:17–18).

Judas, according to Matthew (the only Gospel writer to report this), hanged himself (27:3–5). This act has long been seen as a well-deserved end for the betrayer of Jesus. Some take it as the basis for condemning suicide. Even before Augustine, Petilian had considered Judas's suicide the final act of atonement for his sins, and some have revered Judas for playing a key role in God's plan of salvation. The account of Judas's death in Acts does not refer to his having ended his own life. A strict reading of Matthew's account of Judas's death does not, however, require that it be interpreted as a condemnation of suicide, nor does the story of Judas's gruesome fall in Acts 1:15–18 necessarily presuppose that "the rope broke," as some have assumed.

The most obvious account of an attempted suicide that was thwarted occurs in Acts 16:25–31. Although Paul and his fellow inmates had the opportunity to escape, they did not. The jailer, thinking he had lost his prisoners and fearful of what that would mean for him, was on the verge

of slaying himself when Paul called out to stop him. This
account also has been variously interpreted. Some see it as
an injunction upon Christians to intervene in all suicide
attempts. Others see no such intention, but only Paul's way
of preventing a needless death, even by his persecutor. Still
others see the entire account as part of the author-editor's
depiction of Paul as the evangelist par excellence, who
could use any circumstance, however unlikely or unfortu-
nate, as an opportunity to win converts to his faith in
Christ.

Although he is seldom viewed as a would-be suicide,
Jonah also deserves mention in this connection. No less a
thinker than Nobel laureate Elie Wiesel has written ex-
tensively on the prophet's prolonged suicidal tendencies.
Certainly Jonah's words (1:12) fall into the pattern of suicidal behavior, as it is seen and studied by psychologists,
pastoral counselors, and other professional caregivers
today:

> Take me and throw me into the sea, for I know that it is
> because of me that this trouble has come upon you. Then the
> sea will be quiet for you.

Other accounts of suicide are recorded in postcan-
onical Jewish and Christian writings. As a rule, these
examples are related to military heroes and persecuted
martyrs.

None of these direct accounts are presented as sermons
against suicide, nor are they depicted in such a way as to be
an open invitation to go and do likewise. As has often been
the case, other texts, where suicide is *not* mentioned, have
been used by religious thinkers to condemn the act. Much
less frequently, and always under very restricted circumstances, texts not recording suicide have been used to
condone it.

The word "condone" has a range of meanings that
include to overlook, forgive, excuse, or give tacit approval
to. Nothing said in this book is to be taken to mean that it
implies an advocacy of suicide.

The biblical texts used to condemn or condone suicide

are far too numerous to mention here. They have been assembled and commented on in some of my other writings, included among the references at the end of this book. It will be sufficient here to list only a few of the more common biblical passages used to argue against suicide or to suggest that, under certain carefully prescribed conditions, it could be an option even for a person of genuine faith.

Among the texts used to condemn suicide are the Sixth Commandment, "you shall not kill," or "you shall not commit murder" (Ex. 20:13, Deut. 5:17); "choose life, that you and your descendants may live" (Deut. 30:19); "the LORD gave, and the LORD has taken away" (Job 1:21); "your body is a temple of the Holy Spirit within you" (1 Cor. 6:19); and "no man ever hates his own flesh, but nourishes it and cherishes it" (Eph. 5:28). The persecuted Christians to whom the book of Revelation was addressed were encouraged to hold on a little longer. A repeated theme is that those who endure until the end will receive their rewards (Rev. 3:5, 12, 21; 21:7).

In addition to these and other texts taken as specific injunctions against suicide, there are the personal examples of those who, in spite of intense suffering, refused to take their own lives. Job did not harken to his wife's plea to "curse God and die" (Job 2:9–10). Jesus refused to jump off the pinnacle (Matt. 4:5–7), and Paul, though he longed to depart to be with Christ, opted to stay in order to be of service to those he felt needed him.

Taken together, both the texts seen as specific prohibitions against suicide and those portraying examples of steadfastness in faith regardless of life's oppressive vicissitudes are impressive. Both have appeared frequently in the teachings of synagogues and churches.

The opposite view, however, has also been justified by a rather large number of biblical texts. To be sure, this latter category has not been used frequently, simply because until recently the church did not consider suicide a possible response in faith, and Jewish thought was overwhelmingly opposed to it. Even so, those who read the Bible seek-

ing guidance on this ultimate question are not likely to overlook the possible condoning of suicide in texts
such as John 15:13, which offers the altruistic motive
in Jesus' words: "Greater love has no man than this,
that a man lay down his life for his friends." A similar saying is in the first epistle of John: "By this we know love,
that he laid down his life for us; and we ought to lay down
our lives for the brethren" (3:16). Paul conceded that
"perhaps for a good man one will dare even to die"
(Rom. 5:7).

All these passages and others have been used to condone
suicide in times of extreme persecution, as a form of
self-sacrifice for the good of others, or as an act of ultimate
piety. Clearly, they are not used as a way of encouraging
thoughtless or selfish acts of suicide.

Those who take seriously their method of interpretation
will recognize that several of these are hardly more than
proof texts, used to justify an opinion toward suicide that
does not arise from the text itself. Even so, each text cited
has been used for that purpose within religious circles. The
responsibilities of those who preach on suicide, as on any
other subject, include both examining a text for its inher-
ent meaning and clarifying the basic principles of interpretation. The latter task is especially important for those
prone to read their preconceived notions of suicide into the
Bible.

## Suicide in Religious History

Any introduction to the subject of suicide must rely on
that most comprehensive delineation of its history, the
classic work on suicide, Henry Romilly Fedden's *Suicide: A
Social and Historical Study,* published in 1938. Briefer and
more recent surveys are quite helpful, occasionally adding a
few new facts or insights, but Fedden's work provides the
broadest picture, with hundreds of illustrations and an
excellent description of how the interlocking pieces can be
put together. It deserves at least a quick reading by all

preachers who have yet to preach their first sermon on suicide.

Throughout most of its first three centuries, the church apparently had little to say about suicide one way or the other. But by the year 250, many Christians were accepting the notion that to take one's own life, or to make sure that some oppressor took it for them, was not only an acceptable way to "follow Jesus" but also a sure way to gain martyrdom. In this early period, according to Fedden, "the Church invited massacres when it might have brought off diplomatic victories" (pp. 107–108). Of several pre-Christian arguments against suicide, the early church adopted only one: Plato's notion that to die by one's own hand was as evil as for a soldier to desert his post of duty.

Tertullian of Carthage (160–230) was strong in his advocacy of a self-chosen death, so long as Christians followed Paul's advice in 1 Corinthians 13 to give their bodies to be burned *in love.* He alluded to John's statement that Jesus himself had freely yielded up his spirit to God on the cross. Another of the great Christian preacher-scholar-theologians of that early period, Origen of Alexandria (185?–254?), also held this belief about Jesus' death: that is, that it was voluntarily given, or laid down, *before* it was taken from him.

The appeal of such arguments in the writings of these early church leaders—and, we may well assume, in their preaching—must have been quite strong. In the middle of the fourth century C.E., Augustine (354–430) offered the first full-scale attack on suicide as a sin. Earlier Christians, including Cyprian (c.200–258) and Clement of Alexandria (c.150–215), had argued against suicide on other grounds, but Augustine marshaled all the biblical and theological arguments he could to stem the growing tide of suicide among Christians. In 346, the situation in North Africa prompted the first conciliar action to deny all funeral rites to suicides. That prohibition continued in the Roman Catholic Church until 1983, and some Protestant congregations still follow the old practice.

Fedden insisted that both pre-Christian popular fears of suicide and economic considerations played major roles in the church's growing rigidity against the act. The death of a slave meant a severe loss for the owner and, to some extent, for the state. In a later view, it was also seen as a loss for the kingdom of God on earth. When the numbers grew, the issue could no longer be ignored. Thus the condemnation of suicide was, initially, more of a grass-roots movement than a divine revelation from on high that had to be forced on the masses. It was only later that it caught the attention of church theologians.

In his famous theological work *The City of God,* Augustine detailed four reasons why suicide was not worthy of the Christian. Only one was based specifically on a religious idea. He interpreted the Sixth Commandment to include *self*-murder, which made suicide a direct violation of the most sacred law for Jews and Christians. His other three arguments were derived from what could be called "the world's wisdom." First, he said that to commit suicide is to commit an act that only the state or the church has the right to authorize. Second, he argued that to "escape" the sufferings of this world is an admission of weakness, hence an ignoble act and therefore a refusal to "suffer for Christ's sake." His third argument was prompted by a belief held by certain newly baptized Christians (a group Augustine considered heretical) that it would be better to die while in a state of relative purity than to risk missing heaven altogether through an accumulation of sins in the years ahead. To counter this argument, Augustine insisted that suicide was a greater sin than any they might commit later.

In spite of such forceful arguments by Augustine and others, death through martyrdom continued to be countenanced within the church. In 450 C.E., Christians were still having to be reminded by the historian of Constantinople, Sozomen (c.400–c.450) of "the divine precept which commands us *not to expose ourselves to persecution*" (Fedden, p. 123, italics mine).

Also accepted were deaths from self-inflicted privation by those who deliberately forsook the evils of this world in order to pray and meditate on the life to come. Despair at not being able to live up to exalted ideals of sainthood often prompted a depression so great as to induce suicidal behavior among these devout men and women. Death by starvation was not uncommon.

A third form of suicide frequently accepted was that of women about to lose their virginity or have their marriage violated through forced sexual encounter. Both Ambrose (340?–397) and Jerome (340?–420) expressed their admiration for women who chose to die by their own devices rather than endure such a fate. Conversely, Augustine's views against suicide were so strong that he went to great lengths to show why, even here, suicide was the greater sin. Again from Fedden: "His attack on this sort of suicide ends with the tenuous consolation that such troubles produce humility and are good for the unnatural pride of virgins and chaste women" (p. 132)!

Gradually, as reflected in the records of church councils, the theological arguments against suicide were translated into specific forms of condemnation and punishment. In 563, the Council of Braga prohibited funerals for any suicides, regardless of the circumstances, and in 1284 the Synod of Nîmes refused them burial in a consecrated cemetery.

One slight shift in this steady trend occurred in England and France in the eighth century. Charlemagne's revival of classical thought brought changes throughout the whole society. From a Christian perspective, the Venerable Bede (673–735) restated the understanding that Jesus' death was self-inflicted. Even official guidelines for church response allowed for a quite lenient attitude toward some types of suicide, among them the insane and those possessed of the devil. In some places, funeral rites and burials for known suicides were once again instituted.

After Augustine's strong theological attack on suicide, prompted in large measure by the many suicides of persons claiming to be Christians, the next major discourse by a theologian was that of Thomas Aquinas (1225?–1274). Although their positions were the same, the circumstances for the two thinkers were different. Aquinas was not reacting to a crisis so much as simply addressing one aspect of the larger matter of death in his systematic and comprehensive *Summa Theologica.* This long treatise has been the basis of Christian thought, liturgy, and ethics, especially within Roman Catholicism, for over seven hundred years.

In his methodical argument, Aquinas agreed with Augustine that suicide was a form of self-murder and therefore a violation of the commandment against murder. But his other arguments reflect a greater indebtedness to philosophy—in particular, theories based on natural law—than to the Bible. Suicide, he held, is "unnatural," for according to nature no one would want to do harm to himself or herself. Because the laws of nature were established by God, such an aberrant act must be seen as a sin.

Drawing upon classical Greek philosophy, Aquinas used Aristotle to argue that suicide violated that sense of community of which all persons are a part. Thus, to take oneself voluntarily out of one's community was an affront to society.

A final argument, with biblical overtones, stressed a similar point: A person is not only related to the state but also related to—indeed, *belongs* to—God. Thus, to destroy oneself is to destroy that which belongs to God, and so it is an act of robbery against the Divine. It is easy to see how this notion is rooted in several of those biblical texts that do not make specific reference to a self-chosen death. For example, "The earth is the Lord's and the fulness thereof, the world and those who dwell therein" (Ps. 24:1); and "You are not your own; you were bought with a price" (1 Cor. 6:19–20).

Further, the so-called ransom theory of the atonement, wherein Christ "paid the price" for the salvation of humanity, strengthened the notion that Christians thus redeemed now belong to him. Although some biblical texts are interpreted to support this view, it is clear that the basic argument comes primarily from the realms of natural philosophy and secular economics.

We may pause here to note briefly that in the history of preaching and theologizing on suicide, biblical interpretation has often found its most influential practitioners among poets and dramatists. Dante's *Inferno* not only crystallized opinions of his day but also added one further dimension that has been of lasting consequence—the status of suicides in the underworld. There, people who have killed themselves wail in endless misery, confined to a darkened wood somewhere below heretics and murderers.

Milton's depiction of Adam and Eve and the fall in *Paradise Lost,* and Shakespeare's dramatic portrayals of figures like Richard III and Anthony and Cleopatra, are graphic literary masterpieces. For centuries those poetic characterizations have held sway in the minds of people far more tenaciously than the biblical and historical accounts on which they are based. That is to say, interpretations of the Bible by artists are often more influential than those of theologians, commentators, and preachers! All the more reason, then, for preachers to be aware of the influence of those literary interpretations upon their listeners.

The next major period of church history in which preaching and biblical exposition were at the heart of theological discussion and ethical injunction was the Reformation. Sermons and hymns were as influential among the uneducated masses, who often heard and sang them, as they were among the educated classes, who read treatises and studied commentaries.

Sociologists have long noted the effect of society's structure and values on the individual's behavior. As a rule, the more rigid the structure and the greater one's sense of belonging, the less chance of experiencing the loneliness, depression, or even persecution that often lead to voluntarily removing oneself from that society. The Reformation was a time when many certainties of the Middle Ages were losing their force.

Yet John Calvin's rigid theory of predestination was in

one sense a contributing factor toward a more positive view
of suicide. If a person became convinced that she or he was
among the damned, with no way whatever to earn salvation, then what further fear might suicide bring, either from
the church or state here and now or from divine wrath
hereafter? This assessment of Calvin's theology is clearly
one-sided and is not intended to give a complete understanding of his views. He still had room for personal ethics
and, like his contemporaries, included suicide among the
sins all Christians were to avoid.

Martin Luther seems not to have held a thoroughly
consistent view of suicide. One of my student assistants,
Carole Burnett, noted that in his commentary on Jonah
(1526), Luther called Jonah's desire to end his life, even for
the purpose of ending the storm, "a great sin on the part of
the prophet," although he generally held Jonah in high
regard. In August of the following year, however, a devastating plague struck the city of Wittenberg. Against the
orders of the Elector John to leave, Luther stayed to
minister to the sick. As the plague spread to other cities,
some of the clergy wondered if it was proper to flee from a
deadly plague. Luther responded by saying that one should
stay if service to the neighbor was possible. Preserving one's
own life to avoid risking it in necessary service to others
was not appropriate for the Christian. But if no such
response to help others was possible, then a Christian could
flee in order to escape unnecessary exposure to a life-
threatening disease. Indeed, Luther urged the use of medi-
cines and normal hygiene to avoid the contagion so as not
to tempt God.

In his lectures on Galatians (1535), Luther said that
some people were deceived by the devil into thinking that
Christ himself was urging them to commit suicide. In
the same work he said that the law, apart from grace,
could so condemn people that, in their resultant
despair, many might choose to die by hanging or drown-
ing.

These works show that while Luther saw suicide as a sin,

he could attribute its cause to different sources and be quite tolerant of Jonah in spite of the prophet's suicidal thoughts and behavior. In a letter to Justus Jones, dated December 10, 1527, Luther referred to the well-known suicide of the theologian John Krause. Without condemning Krause, he allowed for the possibility that, even after stabbing himself, the victim may have repented.

This argument has been used at different periods of history among both Jews and Christians: Unless there is irrefutable proof, such as a suicide note, it cannot be assumed that the death was a suicide. Even so, there should be some allowance for a change of heart. Recent psychological studies bear out the presence of much ambiguity among suicide attempts, such as those who have miraculously survived leaps from the Golden Gate Bridge. Suicidologists consider most suicide attempts to be cries for help.

Running contrary to general Reformation and Roman Catholic teachings regarding suicide was the view of the leading humanist of the sixteenth century, Desiderius Erasmus (1466?–1536). Although he never disavowed his Catholicism, Erasmus' classical learning, which had an influence on Luther, led to his reevaluation of suicide. Those who chose death by their own hand to escape the folly of this world were praised for their wisdom. Here again, the source of Erasmus' view lay primarily outside the Bible and theology.

Quite apart from social factors and worldly wisdom, there have been times when ideas of purely theological origin had a significant impact upon society. In 1666 there arose a belief among the Russian populace that the Antichrist was about to appear. Fedden reports (p. 160) that "countless" Christians chose to die through fire and starvation in order to escape the temptation to sin and apostasy which that evil appearance might bring.

As with one's method of biblical interpretation, already mentioned, so with one's choice and treatment of sermon subjects: One must always beware of the extent to which the spirit of the times is influencing one's perspective. Whether the prevailing mood comes from society's grass roots to affect the church or is determined largely by a movement of ideas from the church toward society, the preacher must be able to discern what is going on and to evaluate the results from a perspective that is biblically, historically, and sociologically informed.

Later English clerics, also trained in the classics, occasionally followed the path of Erasmus in expressing an openness to suicide. Among these were Sir Thomas More, Robert Burton, and John Donne.

The most important and cogent work condoning suicide was penned by John Donne, who was dean of St. Paul's in London during the years 1621–1631. Although he never preached on suicide, he wrote an extended treatise arguing that suicide, under certain circumstances, was clearly justified within the Christian faith and that many of the earlier arguments against it were unfounded. That work, *Biathanatos,* he kept a carefully guarded secret, but against his express wishes it was published by his son in 1644, more than a decade after his death. The work was divided into three parts, the last of which drew upon a number of biblical texts, most of them from the Gospel and epistles of John.

With the arrival of the Age of Reason—as the eighteenth century has often been called—suicide, like most every other subject related to human existence, received new scrutiny. This was particularly noticeable in France. Not surprisingly, suicide was viewed by many rationalists as a perfectly legitimate option. If neither society nor the church could provide a meaningful life, then neither could they rightfully condemn those who chose to leave a meaningless one.

Rousseau, through the character of Saint-Preux in *The New Héloïse,* reintroduced a quasi-theological argument among the more popular philosophical ones. Distinguishing clearly between soul and body, he argued that suicide concerned only the latter, which was inferior. Death, even when self-chosen, brought one closer to God.

In this argument one hears, on the one hand, echoes of a rigid dualism that has often been declared heretical; yet, on the other, some familiar themes sounded in Paul and Ignatius, both of whom expressed their strong desires to leave this life to be with Christ. Paul decided to stay; Ignatius preferred to be eaten by the wild beasts in Rome.

In spite of many new works condoning suicide, few eighteenth-century preachers were persuaded to change their views. The famous hymn writer Isaac Watts published a tract in 1726 entitled "A Defense Against the Temptation to Self-Murder. Wherein the Criminal Nature and Guilt of it are display'd . . . Together with Some Reflections on Excess in Strong Liquors, Duelling, and other Practices akin to this heinous Sin." The work, perhaps originally a sermon, examined several biblical texts, including "Thou shalt not kill" (Ex. 20:13) and "I kill and I make alive" (Deut. 32:39).

John Wesley, although he never felt compelled to address the subject in a sermon, expressed his harsh indictment of suicide a short time before his death. Responding to the widespread practice in England in the 1780s, he held that all suicides, of whatever class and presumably for whatever reason, should be treated as in ancient Sparta: that is, they should be publicly exposed. This, he said, would be the surest way to stem the tragic tide of his day.

English clerics of the 1700s were generally opposed to suicide in their writings, although few were as severe as Wesley in their arguments. In February 1805, a Presbyterian minister in New York City, Dr. Samuel Miller, preached two sermons, later published under the title *The Guilt, Folly, and Sources of Suicide.* Both were based on Job 2:9–10, where Job refuses his wife's sarcastic plea for him to curse God and die.

Through much of the nineteenth century, suicide was seldom the occasion for preaching, although it continued to be widely noted by writers, reporters, and those students of human behavior, particularly in France, who were laying the foundation for a new branch of social science to be known as sociology. Convinced that the scholarly world needed a solid, empirically verifiable example of the way social factors determined individual attitudes and behavior, Émile Durkheim published the first major work to demonstrate sociological principles in 1897. To make his case even more forcefully, he chose a subject which, until that time, had been considered the most individualistic act imaginable: suicide. The work not only succeeded in gaining wide acceptance for the new field of study, it also became the classic work for those interested in the study and prevention of suicide. While most sociologists and suicidologists today can no longer accept Durkheim's methods, categories, or conclusions, all acknowledge his seminal role in establishing their fields on a respectable basis.

The significance of sociology and psychology, which came into prominence in the early twentieth century, can hardly be overestimated. More than any other factor, they have caused changes in the way people view the act of self-destruction. In short, the primary effect of these sciences has been to shift the source, or blame, for suicide from the rational individual either to an overpowering set of social factors or to the mysterious inner recesses of the human psyche. By the middle of the present century, most people in religious communities, as well as in society at large, were ready to accept the view that persons who committed suicide were really "beside themselves" and therefore not responsible for their act. This view helped many religious groups to respond to suicide as something other than a personal "sin" and enabled those in the legal profession to see it as something other than a "crime."

More recently, scientists have given strong arguments for the rationality of suicide, and most would agree that persons who take their own lives are not always mentally incompetent. It is this conclusion that has caused a serious rethinking of ethical, philosophical, and theological issues. Is a person rational who chooses to die rather than see a lifetime of earnings go for expensive medical care that could at best extend life for a very short time? Does a person have a basic human right to make such a choice in the light of all carefully considered facts? Can one prize this life so highly that it stands in the way of supreme sacrifice, of all that it was meant to be as service to and for others?

Historical circumstances have also prompted a rethinking of issues related to suicide. Is it more honorable, more "religious," to choose to die in the midst of the Holocaust or to protest an unconscionable war than to continue to live in a situation one cannot morally tolerate but has no way of changing? Are the crudities so explicitly and brazenly expressed in heavy metal music and behavior a contributing factor to a mood of despair and depression? When a thousand teenagers are attempting suicide every day, can the pulpits of America's religious communities continue to keep silent on the issue?

It is this last question that moves us beyond more poetic considerations. The one fact that has prompted so much of the current attention to suicide has been the shift in the statistics among social groups. Few congregations have not been faced with the necessity of rethinking their views on suicide as more and more of their members become victims of this tragic phenomenon. Hardly anyone has not experienced the loss through suicide of a friend, lover, relative, spouse, public servant, entertainment or sports idol, admired community leader, or member of the clergy. When even one person in one of these categories chooses his or her own death, discussion of the issue can be suppressed only at the risk of stifling honest doubt and covering up a host of disturbing emotions that may well come out later in still more debilitating ways.

Facing up to the problems suicide causes within their congregations is an urgent task for preachers, as challenging as it is difficult. But it is one that can be addressed with conviction and confidence. To face these problems will place the preacher well within the noble and historic tradition of those who have been called to relate their faith to all life's vicissitudes.

Lucy Davidson is a psychiatrist in Atlanta, Georgia, who serves as a consultant on suicide to the national Centers for Disease Control, one of two government agencies charged with the prevention of suicide. In May 1987 she addressed a working conference of United Methodist leaders who were attempting to write that denomination's first official statement on suicide. Dr. Davidson cited four important areas where religious leaders need to be involved: (1) clergy and church-related counselors are often first to be sought out for help by suicidal persons, sometimes by those suffering from religious delusions; (2) they can help demolish the myths of suicide, such as that "talking about suicide will only plant the idea"; (3) they can refrain from glorifying victims of suicide, especially at funerals; and (4) they can address the needs of caregivers themselves in times of crisis. Each of these special forms of ministry requires much study and skill, which can come only when suicide is taken seriously by religious communities.

Sociologists, psychiatrists, and others in the field of suicidology are convinced that more open discussion is very much needed to turn the tide. Evangelist Jerry Johnston addresses thousands of high school students each year. In his very informative and poignant book *Why Suicide?* he says (p. 126):

> Suicidologists . . . are in nearly universal agreement that talking about this disturbing issue does not prompt people to take their lives. In fact, discussion is one of the most important deterrents.

Johnston is convinced that this is one of the major myths to be done away with. "Just knowing that others are struggling, too, helps immeasurably in a teenager's ability to cope."

This survey should be of benefit to those who would preach on suicide or who want to know more of what religious leaders have thought, preached, and advocated over the centuries. It should also provide a good point of reference in reading the sermons that follow, all by preachers who are openly addressing the matter of suicide today.

*James T. Clemons* is Professor of New Testament at Wesley Theological Seminary in Washington, D.C., where he has taught for twenty-one years. He holds degrees from Hendrix College, Southern Methodist University, and Duke University. His teaching and lecturing in the field of suicide have been conducted in several states, and he is the author of seven articles on the subject.

This sermon was preached at the request of a student pastor who at the time was serving his first appointment. During one Lenten season, his congregation focused its studies and worship on death and dying. The student had found little understanding of the social, ethical, and theological dimensions of the problem, even though there had been four recent suicides within the community.

# 1

# Death by Choice
## *1 Samuel 31:1–13; Mark 8:31–35*

## James T. Clemons

When Christians begin their Lenten pilgrimage, the themes of death and dying, life and living, are constantly before us. From the start of the journey, from whatever town or village, whatever suburb or inner city we happen to be in at the moment, we know where it will end—at the foot of the cross and at the empty tomb, just outside Jerusalem.

Along the way, we explore many facets of the meaning of Jesus' death. We ask about his choice of death, and about the circumstances of his times. And then we ask about our choices, in the midst of the circumstances surrounding us.

As responsible Christians, we are called in this Lenten journey to ask, How does our faith in Jesus Christ relate to all areas of our lives, including our own view of death?

As we come to this particular Lenten season—as Christians in America, as members of a particular community and local church, and as members of particular families and groups of friends—in all these several relationships, we come now to worship and to examine our faith.

## Statistics

You have decided to focus in these forty days on the meaning of death and dying, and this morning we shall be confronting one of the most tragic aspects of that broad issue, suicide.

In order to see how this tragic reality affects our lives—as citizens, as members of this community, with particular families and friends—we should begin by noting some of the awesome statistics that confront us.

• The most rapid increase over the past two years has been among our teenagers and young adults. It is estimated that some 5,000 young people will die by suicide this year, and that at least one hundred times that many will attempt it.

• The highest rate of suicide for any age group in the United States is among the elderly.

• Other statistics reveal that there has been a phenomenal increase in the number of suicides among blacks and among prison inmates.

• We are reminded that three times as many women attempt suicide as men, but three times as many men succeed.

• And we are told that psychologists now speak of "early onset depression," which is often seen in suicidal children as early as age three.

Such statistics within our society make it clear that suicide is a concern for all of us and one that calls for a Christian response, both from the church as a whole as well as from its individual members. Unfortunately there is no easy answer, in spite of the fact that the church has for so long had only one position. It is time for us to rethink what our faith has to say.

## Our Theological Task

Many people in the church have the notion that theology is something that is to be left to the seminaries and schools of theology. But I want to give a simple definition which I believe shows that doing theology is every Christian's responsibility and, in fact, is something we are all engaged in most of the time.

This definition comes out of an adult Sunday school class my wife and I attend. It is simply: Faith is a gift. (Paul said this in his epistles.) *Theology is our effort to understand the Giver, the gift, and the implications of its acceptance.* That is to say, God has given us the gracious gift of life, and theology is the attempt to know what it means to live out of the awareness that this gift of life is ours, both to enjoy and to use responsibly.

Methodists are given four basic guidelines to use in going about their theological task. These four are derived from the way John Wesley went about his thinking on the Christian faith and its application to life. These four guidelines are: scripture, tradition, experience, and reason. Each one has something to say to us as we rethink the meaning of our faith in relation to this important concern about suicide.

### Scripture

Although the Bible has several passages that speak to us about suicide, the two I have chosen as our texts for the day are not often cited.

One of the great Old Testament figures is Saul, the first king of Israel. Before his day, you may recall, the people of Israel had refused to have a king of their own. Their religious belief was that only God was their king, and that to have a human king was nothing less than a form of idolatry.

In times of danger from their enemies, the several tribes would simply get together and go out to fight the necessary battle. Then they would go back to their own fields. We can see that such a form of national defense would not really work too well.

Eventually, and only after much strong objection, Israel decided to have a permanent king, with the authority to form a standing army and to secure the necessary ways and means of maintaining it.

The accounts in 1 Samuel tell us of the selection of Saul to be the first king and of his long career. That part of the Old Testament ends with the story of his being wounded by the Philistines, of his defeat, and of his final choice of suicide.

Obviously, both Saul and his armor-bearer chose death by their own hands rather than submit to the Philistine army. It is interesting to note that in this account, there is not the slightest hint that Saul or his armor-bearer were to be condemned for their behavior.

Furthermore, whenever Saul is later referred to by other Old Testament writers, there is no suggestion that he did anything wrong in the way he died. What this shows is that the Old Testament does not give an out-and-out condemnation of suicide in every form.

The passage from the Gospel of Mark (8:31–35) gives us Jesus' own words as to what he expects of his followers. In that passage, Jesus' words have been presented in a unique way. It challenges its readers to ask, What does it mean to follow Jesus in our particular circumstances? The answer is given in the clearly stated challenge: *Take up your cross!*

Those first Christians would have understood what this meant. Many were ready to give up their lives, *to choose death*—by whatever horrible form the Roman rulers might conceive—in order to be faithful to both the command and the example of Christ.

Here again, then, there is no condemnation of those who would deliberately choose death for the sake of being true to their faith. And indeed, in the very early centuries of the Christian church, those who did choose death in this way were considered saints, not sinners. To take up one's cross meant to be ready to choose death, when necessary, in order to be true to one's faith.

As we look at these two passages in particular, we see that the Old and New Testaments both give us a different viewpoint on suicide than we are accustomed to hearing. If we were to take other passages, even those that have been singled out to show that the Bible condemns suicide, we would find that they are often less clear on the matter than we have been led to believe.

The point here is that the Bible, when read from cover to cover and when taken honestly in terms of *all* that it has to say on the subject, does not present us with an outright condemnation of self-chosen death. There are different points of view within the Bible, and as we make use of scripture in going about our theological task, we need to look carefully at all the points of view which the Bible has to offer on the subject.

### Tradition

The second guideline for our thinking on the meaning of faith is tradition. By this we mean what the church has taught over some twenty centuries. Much of the two-thousand-year history, of course, was shaped by the thousands of years of Israelite and Jewish religious thought that preceded the founding of the church. As I mentioned, in the early centuries, death by choice was often preferred if the only alternative was to renounce or to hide one's faith in Christ.

It was not until the time of Augustine in the fourth century that the position against suicide was set forth by a major theologian and widely accepted within the church. Augustine was one of the church's greatest thinkers, and he had a tremendous influence on both Martin Luther and John Wesley. It was his view that the Sixth Commandment, "Thou shalt not murder," included a prohibition against self-murder. After his time, Christians generally came to accept this negative view.

In the twelfth century another great theologian, Thomas Aquinas, reinforced this notion. He appropriated the philosophical thought of the ancient Greek philosopher Aristotle and applied it to Christian faith and morals. Among other things, Aquinas believed that whatever was to be seen in nature was good: that is, it was what God intended it to be.

And, because it is not natural for a creature to kill itself, so it is not natural for any human to kill himself or herself. Thus, he reasoned, it was against God's natural law to commit suicide.

Five hundred years later, in seventeenth-century England, one of the better known English divines wrote a treatise against the long-held view that suicide was always wrong. That man was John Donne, who is best remembered for his statement, "No man is an island." But Donne's arguments amounted to very little, and the church's long-held position remained the dominant one.

In the eighteenth century, John Wesley subscribed whole-heartedly to the traditional view. In spite of the fact that he had been at the forefront of many progressive ideas involving prison reform, emancipation from slavery, employment, education, and medical care for the poor, Wesley wrote as late as 1790 a scathing denunciation of what he called "self-murder." He offered as the final solution one of the most hideous forms of retribution to be imagined. If all Methodists had to subscribe to Wesley's own view on that subject, hardly anyone would remain in the denomination.

Now I would be safe in saying, I'm sure, that most of the adults here have grown up believing that *the* Christian attitude toward suicide is that it is a sin and, perhaps, that those who died by their own hand had forfeited any chance of receiving God's forgiveness for that act. This in turn meant that they were going straight to hell.

Again, what we learn from a look at tradition is that the church has had different views on the subject over the course of its long history. Further, we see from such a study that, at each crucial point, specific circumstances entered into the decision about what *the* Christian position should be. Sometimes these influences were factors related to how the Bible was interpreted, often just one verse, and at other times they were prompted by certain philosophical ideas that came from outside the Bible.

## Experience

A third guideline to use in thinking theologically is experience. This, of course, is a word with a wide range of meanings. For Wesley, it most often meant the inner experience a person had that bore witness to the Spirit of God, which one could know in one's heart. This was the basic intent when John Wesley spoke of his "heartwarming experience" at Aldersgate in 1738.

But there were also other dimensions of the term "experience," even for Wesley. These included the clear demonstration by others that God was at work in their lives. Wesley was by nature very conservative. But once he saw, through the experience of others, what was clearly God's work and will, he then acted in response to this experience to make changes in his own beliefs and in his administration of the early Methodist societies.

We have but to recall his decision to permit lay Methodists to preach, his decision to begin preaching in the fields when the pulpits of the Church of England were closed to him, and his final decision to allow the Methodists of America to organize their own church. He also changed his mind with regard to his use of scripture and his belief in the assurance that a person could know of (experience) the forgiveness of God.

What this helps us to see is that both the personal experience and the collective experience of Christians in any age are important factors to be considered in determining what our faith means in given situations.

When we come to the matter of suicide, we see that human experience is broad enough to include a wide range of thought and action regarding how we are to view suicide in general, as well as how we are to respond to the experience of others, even, I believe, those outside the church and members of other faith communities.

That is to say, as we experience the pain and loss and grief, and often the guilt, that comes with suicide, and, yes, the anger and alienation and the tendency to blame ourselves and others, then we are forced to ask ourselves, What does this kind of common human experience teach us as Christians?

Experience, both personal and collective, within both church and society, is also to be considered whenever we seek to deal with a major problem involving Christian faith and life.

### Reason

One of the strongest factors in John Wesley's thinking about faith and life was reason. As you may recall from history, the eighteenth century was a time when pretty much all of Europe, but especially England, was struggling with the challenges of a new way of thinking. It tended to question every tenet and authority, whether political, moral, social, or religious.

It was a time when the church and Christian beliefs particularly were being challenged, and as a result many religious folk were opposed to the use of reason in religious thought. Indeed, Martin Luther was exceedingly suspicious of any reliance upon human reason, even though he himself was quite logical and believed strongly in secular learning in order to understand scripture.

But John Wesley, conservative though he was in many ways, always put the highest premium upon reason, upon the full use of our minds, including the broadest possible study of so-called secular learning. He believed, as did the ancient Greeks, that it was one of God's greatest gifts to humanity. In this respect, as in several others, he was strongly influenced by his mother, Susannah.

So, the fourth guideline Methodists are called upon to follow in doing theology is the use of reason. Of course, what is reasonable to one can easily seem sheer nonsense to another. That is why, in the last analysis, we are to use all four guidelines and to do our theologizing together. We move toward a common understanding of what our faith means in the light of any one particular circumstance, such as suicide.

All of this brings us, then, to take a closer look at the tragic matter that confronts our church and our society today. It is a tragedy that affects all segments of our national life. We know that many of the attitudes that affect our relationships with families and friends of suicides, our care for suicidal persons, our social customs, and even our laws, have been formed by the teachings of the church.

But today, even within the church, attitudes are changing, and laws within society are also changing. Many of you will recall that, for decades, if any Roman Catholic died by suicide the body was not permitted to be buried in a church cemetery, nor could a final funeral mass be offered. Many Protestants shared that belief, even if the practice was not formally prescribed. But what heartrending suffering this situation caused the family and friends of the deceased! What bitterness toward the church often lingered, sometimes years after the burial! And what callous lack of concern resulted in terms of pastoral care from the minister or church members in view of this attitude!

It is here, within the area of the church's need to reach out to those who are suffering, in the area of genuine pastoral care, that I think our attention to suicide can have its greatest positive value.

But we can also bear more of a Christian witness if we take the matter seriously enough to ask, Is there any way we can help turn the tide of so many wasted lives among the young and the elderly and blacks and prison inmates (often first-time offenders) and military personnel and women and professional people and laborers and career people from all walks of life? We have a responsibility to get involved, as citizens, as family members and neighbors, and as Christians. We need to know what is going on, and we must be ready to give of ourselves to meet the needs of others, to be informed, to be interested, to be involved.

## Conclusion

This brings us back to the meaning of Lent and how our reflection of Jesus' death and dying can bring life and living.

Our faith is centered on the belief that because Jesus chose death on our behalf, we have been given new life. In the words of Jesus, recorded in John's Gospel, he came that we might have life and have it more abundantly!

Each time we read of a suicide, regardless of who or where, it is a challenge to us to ask, Where has the church failed to bring that abundant life which would have turned that particular tragedy into a blessing for the individual and perhaps for all humanity?

Jesus asked us to take up our cross. We know that through all of his journey, the hilltop cross ever loomed before him. And as we make our way through these forty days, that cross is ever before us as well, reminding us that through him we have received the gift of life, abundant life, and that we are called to do all we can to bring abundant life to others.

God is gracious and good. God strengthens and encourages and guides us, through all the difficult circumstances of life. We know that we are forgiven, and accepted, and loved, in spite of all we have done and think and are.

We grieve over each suicide. We grieve for each family member and friend who survives. We grieve for our nation, and for all the nations of the world. But we do not shy away from reality. We are called to respond in love and caring and tenderness and with all the resources of our minds and hearts to bear witness to the saving grace of Jesus Christ, whose death by choice has enabled us, and all human beings, to live. Our Lenten worship and reflection thus leads us to choose life, in the name and for the sake of Jesus Christ.

***W. Guy Delaney*** is pastor of the Presbyterian Kirk in the Pines, Hot Springs Village, Arkansas. Before assuming this post in June 1988, he served as Director of Continuing Education and Doctor of Ministry Studies at Union Theological Seminary in Virginia.

This sermon was preached at Trinity Presbyterian Church in Arlington, Virginia, where he served as pastor before joining the faculty at Union Seminary. The sermon was later used in a seminar on teenage suicide at Westbrook Hospital in Richmond, Virginia, on April 24, 1984, for a group of religious professionals. Its intention was to break with the traditional negative position the church has taken on suicide by affirming God's ultimate claim on us, a claim that cannot be overridden by any human act. The language of the sermon is direct, and the word "suicide" is deliberately used more than once, not to stress the act but to disarm the power with which our silence has invested it. Its purpose was to open the dialogue between the church and the world on one of the most troubling issues facing the young in our society.

# 2

# God's Ultimate Claim
### *Romans 14:5–9*

## W. Guy Delaney

It is not easy for us to conceive a more melancholy moment than the one we now share, sitting together at the edge of understanding, attempting to find some answer, some human meaning in the silence of someone who was precious to us and is gone. We come to this sad moment bewildered by what has happened but also ill prepared, because it was so totally unexpected and so ultimately final. The grim reality that grips us has left our senses numbed and our ability to think confused. Suddenly life is not what we expected or thought we had a right to hope it would be.

It seems so inappropriate for us to say we knew John, to speak of him in the past tense. But that is part of our new reality: We did know John. We know his Christian name was John David, the name used in his baptism which links him to Jesus Christ. We know that he would have been seventeen years old if he had lived until March 21. We know that he was a junior at the local high school, that he was an average student, and that he was a member of the track team. We knew his love for animals, his taste for pizza, and his distaste for affluence. We knew him as a son, as a brother, and as a friend. Yes, we knew John. What we don't know is why he took his own life.

Why? This is the question we are all asking ourselves and

one another. If we could only answer this question, some-how our grief might be more bearable, somehow our guilt might not rise up and accuse us so arrestingly, somehow the gloom that hangs over us like a starless night might be lifted. Why? It is so natural for us to ask this question, as if its answer could release us from the ache of John's death.

But, my friends, the answer to this nagging question that goes on repeating itself in our thoughts and our conversa-tions would not satisfy our heart's desire. To know why would solve very little. An answer would only give rise to the same question. No reason would be enough to set our minds at ease. No reason why would return sparkle to our eyes and laughter to our voices.

But if we cannot know why, what questions can we ask and what answers can we expect? Some questions we hesitate to ask for fear of the answers we may get, and some answers we give are worse than no answers. Any one of us might give the answer that was given to a Frenchman who, at the turn of the century, went to a physician and said, "Doctor, you've got to help me. I can't go on with life. Please help me end it all." And the doctor said, "Now, now, my friend, you musn't talk that way. You must laugh and smile and enjoy life. Make friends. Mix with people. Why not go to the circus tonight and see the great clown Debereau? He will make you laugh and forget your trou-bles." The man looked into the face of the physician with his sad eyes and said in a painful whisper, "But, doctor, I am Debereau."

The right questions that are often left unasked and the wrong answers that surround the lives of people like Debereau take their toll among us. Our own feelings of inadequacy and the fear of asking or saying the wrong thing often force us into silence. It is a painful thing to struggle with the issues of suicide. It is even more painful when we are as preoccupied with it as we are in this moment. The word itself, if spoken at all, may be spoken only in a sigh. The sense of shame, the burden of failure, the feelings of guilt, the look on our faces of hopelessness, the grief of loss—all, like waves, wash over us, tossing us back and forth between anger and despair.

What, then, can we say? We are not the first people ever to come face to face with the stark reality of our finitude. It was Paul who long ago cried out for release from life that seemed hemmed in on all sides. "Who will deliver me from this body of death?" he said. And before these words could fade into silence, he answered his own question with a doxology: "Thanks be to God through Jesus Christ our Lord" (Rom. 7:24–25).

What is it that allows Paul to give thanks on every occasion? Is it not the belief that God's claim for each one of us is ultimate, that nothing can separate us from the love of God—not death, not life, not angels, not principalities, not things present, not things to come, not powers, not heights, not depths, not anything—not even suicide.

It is true. The church has not always affirmed that God's grace can reach behind every event to the person, that God can rescue us from this body of death even when that death comes from our own hands. Our attitude about suicide often springs from presuming to know more about God than we actually are capable of knowing. What we have let our attitude and lack of charity do in the case of suicide is reach conclusions that our faith will not support. We must never forget that the Christian faith itself originated in an act of willing acceptance of death, a death which, we say, atoned for the sins of others. We must ever remember that Jesus taught his followers that their death, when done for the sake of a friend, was an expression of the highest form of love.

It was a long, long time ago, to be sure, but there was a time when, because of Jesus' own acceptance of his death, many of his followers willed their own death and even sought it. The people are known to us as martyrs, but, what is more important, many of them now carry the title "Saint" in front of their name. We are tempted to make a distinction between the will and the deed, between the desire and the act, but in so doing we should be aware that Jesus refused such distinctions.

None of this should be understood as counseling others to go and do likewise. Suicide is a very serious, irreversible act. But it is not the sin that many want to make it. If it were, we are all to be pitied, because deep within each one of us, as far away from our own consciousness as denial can keep it, is a profound yearning for death. Many things in life awaken a longing for death in each one of us, which is why suicide, according to Paul Tillich, "actualizes an impulse latent in all life. This is the reason for the presence of suicidal fantasies in most people."[1]

And so, my friends, I use this occasion with some sense of inappropriateness, at the death of one of God's children and a member of our Christian family, whom we love and will see no more, to affirm the value of John's life to us and to God, if not to John himself. We cannot know all the circumstances that surrounded John's decision to end his life, but we can know this: "None of us lives to himself, and none of us dies to himself. If we live, we live to the Lord, and if we die, we die to the Lord; so, then, whether we live or whether we die, we are the Lord's. For to this end Christ died and lived again, that he might be Lord both of the dead and of the living" (Rom. 14:7–9).

"Thanks be to God, who gives us the victory through our Lord Jesus Christ" (1 Cor. 15:57).

---

[1] Paul Tillich, *Systematic Theology* (Chicago: University of Chicago Press, 1963), vol. 3, p. 57.

*William A. Holmes* is Minister of Preaching and Administration of the Metropolitan Memorial United Methodist Church in Washington, D.C. He holds academic degrees from Hendrix College and Southern Methodist University and has done graduate study at Union Theological Seminary in New York City. He has written articles for more than a dozen periodicals and one book, *Tomorrow's Church: A Cosmopolitan Community* (1968).

This sermon was preached by Dr. Holmes to the congregation at Metropolitan Memorial Church on June 22, 1986, after he had been invited by two congregations in Dover, Delaware, to address the subject because of recent suicides among young people there. In conjunction with the sermon, Dr. James Clemons lectured on the subject, and then the two ministers met informally with persons who wanted to pursue the subject further.

# 3

# Fifty Thousand
# Suicides a Year!

## William A. Holmes

We are a nation where a person is more likely to take his or her own life than to be killed by someone else. Fifty thousand suicides a year and growing means that every twelve months we lose more persons to self-inflicted deaths than we lost in the entire Vietnam War.

The news media of late have reminded us of the alarming acceleration of suicides among adolescents. And the largest number of suicides of any group in America today continues to be—as it has been for quite some time—among the old. In the course of a lifetime almost every family in America will be touched by this phenomenon: the suicide of either a family member or a friend. Every minister must deal with this pastoral concern, for every congregation has within its midst persons whose lives have been touched by the poignant and grim reality that is the subject of this sermon.

Let us consider first the phenomenon of suicide through biblical and historical perspectives, and then move to more contemporary, vanguard reflections.

The event of suicide is explicitly mentioned only six times in the Bible. In the Old Testament there is the reference to King Saul (and his armor-bearer) falling upon his sword rather than being taken captive by the Philistines. There is the story of the blind giant, Samson, pulling down the columns of the Temple and killing with his own death more people than he had killed throughout his lifetime. There are three other references to the suicides of minor characters in the Old Testament, and in the New Testament there is the familiar story of Judas Iscariot betraying our Lord and then going out and hanging himself.

In the early years of the church, suicide was forbidden and looked upon as a sin. However, it was an act for which some exceptions were granted. Josephus, one of the authors of early stories about Christian martyrs, has in one of his books the story of a mother and her two virtuous daughters who were captured by lustful soldiers. Rather than submit, the three women hurled themselves into the river. This was a time in history when virtue was considered more precious than life itself.

By the fourth century, Augustine, bishop of Hippo, was writing that the commandment "Thou shalt not kill" applies as much to oneself as it does to one's enemies. Even so, Augustine went on to allow for times when a person could be convinced in conscience that taking one's own life was the will of God. In the years that followed, Thomas Aquinas wrote that there could be no exceptions to justify suicide. It was the one unforgivable sin because it precluded any opportunity for repentance. Dante continued this theme in the *Inferno.* He put people who take their own lives at the seventh level of hell, even beneath murderers. For centuries the Roman Catholic Church refused to allow the bodies of suicide victims to be buried in cemeteries consecrated by the church.

In the seventeenth century a famous Anglican preacher by the name of John Donne argued that under certain circumstances suicide could even be a noble and gracious act. He quoted the words from the New Testament, "Greater love hath no man than that he lay down his life for his friends."

In brief, the church's position has varied from a hard-line insistence that suicide is the unforgivable sin, without exception, to a position of arguing for suicide under certain circumstances—especially when offered as a sacrifice on behalf of other persons. The bottom line is that we are still struggling in the Christian community with the complex and agonizing issue of what it means to take one's own life.

In a contemporary context, the issue of suicide must be considered in relation to modern science and the capacity of medical technology to extend life almost ad infinitum. We can now keep people alive under circumstances that some would call a living death.

I should add that, among all the experts I have read on this subject, there is a clear consensus that a person who is terminally ill and considering suicide should share that consideration with his or her family, friends, minister or priest or rabbi, and trusted medical personnel, so that the decision is made within a network of as much objectivity and love as possible.

Within the last twelve months, I have been with a family in my church—standing with them around a bed in an intensive care unit, holding the hand of a father and husband. He had previously indicated he did not want to be kept alive by machines. We complied. As we stood around that bed together holding hands, we recited aloud the Twenty-third Psalm. The respirator was turned off and we gave thanks for his life, we gave thanks for his death, and we gave thanks for his life eternal. Medical technology, with its bitterest capacity to extend sick life, has, for all its benefits, created a new context in which to consider the willing of one's own death in relation to a terminal condition.

Now let me ask you to move from the vanguard and the prophetic to the pastoral. I refer, with profound concern, to the tragically increasing rate of suicides among adolescents in our day. The rate has tripled in the last three decades, and now, on the average, thirteen young people in America take their lives each day.

A part of the problem is with the older generation, our selective memories of our own teenage years, and our denial of problems. We have a tendency to romanticize the teenage years as being euphoric and without problems. But a recent study shows that in the normal life cycle of a person, feelings of isolation, loss, and stress are never greater than around age sixteen. It is as traumatic as it is normal to move from the securities of childhood to the insecurities of adolescence and adulthood. In the process, one experiences body chemistries heretofore unknown, along with a variety of new feelings and emotions. It is wrenching to begin to transfer one's emotional dependency from one's parents to one's peers, and on occasions to be found living in a world where adults expect teenagers to act like adults while treating them like children. And a part of the problem is the denial of adults who don't want to hear or think about the teenage years in terms of stress and pain.

Another part of the problem is with our culture and its preoccupation with short-term solutions and instant fixes. One child psychologist has said that when children and young people grow up in a society watching hundreds of thousands of hours of television where problems are solved within thirty-minute frames of reference, the young soon come to the conclusion that that's the way life is. They expect short-term solutions and instant fixes for the problems of their own lives, some of them turning to drugs and alcohol for help. Our sons and daughters are simply reflecting the superficial and simplistic goals, values, and priorities of our society itself.

Before someone stands and cries, "Physician, heal thyself," let me admit that a part of the problem is also the church. The subject of suicide is almost taboo with us, and it is extremely hard for us to even begin considering the church's role in combating the escalating tragedy of hopelessness and despair among our youth.

What would it mean for the church to become a place where its sons and daughters could feel that they could really be themselves? A place where you don't have to put on airs, you don't have to be a goody-goody? A place where you can talk about what's real in life, including your own sense of pain or loneliness or isolation? What would it mean for a community of faith to quite intentionally plan intergenerational events where the young of the church could feel at home and know that they were really wanted? This would have to include the hour of worship on Sunday morning: not only a time for children and youth to serve as acolytes, ushers, greeters, and lay readers but also a time when some of their music would be heard and some of their language spoken. Does the litmus test on Sunday morning really have to be the clothes that people wear? What does it mean to communicate, "We're glad to have you regardless of what you're wearing"?

It's time for each congregation to do its homework on the phenomenon of suicide in such a way as to be able to debunk the mythologies and half-truths that so easily swirl about this subject. One such myth is: "Suicidal tendencies are inherited and passed on genetically in the bloodstream from one generation to the other." That's just not true. Or there is the half-truth that anyone who has ever contemplated suicide is mentally ill. Some people who are mentally ill commit suicide, true, but some people contemplate suicide simply because at a given moment in their lives they are nearly overwhelmed by emotional stress and pain. That's a normal part of what it means from time to time to be a human being. Another half-truth is, "If a person is going to commit suicide, they're going to commit suicide and there's nothing anyone can do about it." That's baloney. Lots of people have contemplated suicide, talked about it, and decided against it, because some of the people who heard them talking reached out to them, offered them support and love, and made an extraordinary difference.

It is time for every congregation, whenever a suicide occurs, to be sure that those who are touched by guilt and pain, a sense of sorrow and isolation, know that there are others who stand beside them and with them, offering their own tears and love.

If a part of the problem is the church, then, by the grace of God, a part of the solution can also be the church.

With this I close. Kathleen Housley is a member of a congregation that has a drama group for teenagers. One

Sunday evening, the congregation was invited to a play put on by that drama group entitled "Quiet Cries," from the Plays for Living series, written and produced under the auspices of the Family Service Association of America. "In the play three [teenagers] contemplate committing suicide for quite different reasons. The 'quiet cries' they make, both verbal and behavioral, also vary. . . . Their behavior includes withdrawal, marked personality change, and the giving away of valued possessions." At the beginning of the play it is indicated that one of the characters, not identified, will actually commit suicide. The audience must decide who it is. And Kathleen Housley adds, "This situation made for a very lively debate following the performance. The audience was divided into discussion groups, led by social workers, counselors, and nurses, who helped the group identify the quiet cries and the people who were in a position to hear them."[1]

Friends, we don't have a play to accompany this sermon, but I daresay each of us has a drama being acted out right now in our own families or schools or neighborhoods, or offices, or in this congregation. What would it mean for us to get ears in our ears and to be found listening for quiet cries? How about the church of Jesus Christ as an ICU, an intensive care unit, *before* and not just *after* the tragic fact of suicide?

Let us pray. Almighty God, Father and Mother of us all, loving each of us as though we are your only child while loving us all the same, help us, when we are old, to move with confidence and trust toward the valley of the shadow. And help us, when we are young, to cling to life, even with its pain, because of family and friends and congregations who believe in us and help us to understand the precious persons that we are to them and you. In the name of Him who gave up his life to make that clear. Amen.

---

[1] Kathleen Housley, *The Christian Century*, April 30, 1986, p. 439.

*Madeline Jervis* is pastor of Clarendon Presbyterian Church in Arlington, Virginia. After a first career as a mother and homemaker, she earned her degree at American University. Because she then felt called to the ministry, she attended Wesley Theological Seminary and was ordained shortly after she graduated.

This sermon was preached at the regular worship service following a highly publicized suicide by a well-known church leader. Because of the publicity surrounding the suicide and the intense emotions in the congregation and community, she believed the subject should be addressed publicly in a pastoral and theological context.

# 4

# Sins and Spirit

## *1 Kings 19:15–21;*
## *Galatians 5:1, 13–26*

## Madeline Jervis

As I cast about for scripture for this Sunday, I kept coming back to the lectionary texts. It had seemed to me again
this week that I could not possibly resume the series on Galatians that I had begun after Pentecost. When I looked
at the passage for today, it seemed to be out of the question. It is the beginning of the ethical teachings of the
letter to the Galatians. After preaching the grace of God
and the freedom of the gospel, Paul reminds the churches
that because they had been freed from law, therefore
they must live in a way that demonstrates their new
condition.

At first it seemed to me that a catalog of sins and an
inventory of the fruits of the Spirit would have nothing to
say to us as we continue to mourn the death of our friend.
But then, as I looked through the Bible, seeking inspiration
(or even a workable idea), I kept coming back to the
assigned text, not in its particulars but in its overall
message.

In this passage Paul is talking about community. The sins
he lists are not the beginning of a new set of prohibitions, a
new code of "thou shalt nots," but a listing, by no means
comprehensive, of those things that break Christian fellow-
ship. Paul lists those acts and feelings that break the bonds

of trust that allow us to live in peace with each other, the sins that make us unable to live in peace with God.

With the suicide of our friend, the fabric of our community is damaged. The allegations of sexual irregularities with children that we have been reading about in the papers have torn it. What can we believe about each other if these stories are true? How can we have known someone so long and not known how bitterly unhappy he was?

All of this has hurt us badly, as individuals and in our life together as a community of faith. Are we really a community, members of the body of Christ? Or are we a company of strangers? What can we believe or say now about ourselves?

To begin with, I want to share with you a brief summary of what I know, and what I guess, as a result of all the events of the past ten days. I have talked to friends and strangers, to the police, to the human services people in our county, and I have read the papers as you have.

First of all, I want to say absolutely and without equivocation that our friend helped many, many young people in his life. He helped them and never harmed them. I have talked to some of them and to their parents. Some of them are known to you. To keep perspective, it is important to remember this.

Because he was so involved in the lives of his students, perhaps inappropriately sometimes, the police and the school system investigated him at various times. Rightly so. We entrust our children to our schools and teachers. It is important that our trust and our children are not abused. As far as I have been able to find out, no evidence was ever found in these investigations of criminal behavior that would warrant arrest or even dismissal.

In the week before his death, a specific complaint of abuse was made and the police tell me they were preparing to arrest him. It is difficult to think that this was true. It is even harder to bear the possibility that we will never know what really happened.

No charges will now be filed. There will be no trial, no opportunity to look at the evidence, no chance to test the veracity of the complaint, no chance for our friend to defend himself. Even as we affirm the innocence of the accused person, until proven guilty, there is a worm of doubt gnawing at our minds, and particularly with such an inflammatory issue. We are left with heavy hearts and no real answers.

My guess is that our friend's suicide had to do with his potential arrest. Innocent or guilty, probably he would have lost his teaching credentials, and perhaps it was this possibility he could not bear.

There is a dynamic of death that enters in when suicide is contemplated, a dynamic that narrows focus, that blocks out reason and hope. We cannot know, really, why our friend did this, only that he believed there was no other way out. I am sure he had no idea how much hurt he would cause by his action.

I am talking about these painful things now because it has been a community event, reported in the paper and talked about privately. It is no secret, and to treat it as a secret now would harm us more. Our friend's death and its attendant commotion have alarmed us and hurt us. Before we can begin to recover, before we can begin to mend the rip in the fabric of our community, we have to acknowledge what has happened, name the reality of it, admit our pain.

As we do this, we do not need to assign blame to anyone, or even to pass judgment, as Paul does so easily in our lesson. Judgment belongs to God, who has mercy enough and justice enough for all of us. Whatever our friend did or did not do in this life, he is beyond human justice now and in the hands of God.

When we mend a garment, we have to look it over to see how bad it is before we know how to fix it. When we bandage a wound, we first look it over and clean it up before we slap on the gauze pad. And so, as we begin to heal our life together, we need to talk about what is going on. This is not scandalmongering or gossip. This is our common life, what is happening to us. We need to be able to grieve together, to talk about our fears and anger, to say how we are feeling and what we are thinking.

Our lesson from 1 Kings is also about community. Israel has been suffering under a faithless king. Elijah has run away to the desert, threatened with death by Jezebel the queen; he has despaired of any hope being left for Israel. But God calls Elijah out of the cave where he has been hiding and tells him to start over. All is not lost, and God will protect and save the faithful remnant of Israel. It was a community that had suffered far more grievous trials than we have, but for them, too, there was hope and a promise of a new day.

I know we would rather run away, hole up, than face what has been happening. These past ten days have been awful for all of us. I know we have all been grieving with tears, and sleepless nights, and stomachaches, and all the other ways we respond to stress. There hasn't been a day when I have not wished myself far away. I know we don't want to hear any more about it. We would rather pretend it's all over and never mention these awful days and nights again.

It is our fears that keep us separated, silenced, so that we do not know how others are suffering too, so that we do not know that our doubts and hopes are shared by many. It is our human connections that bring us life, and sanity, and the relief that comes when our isolation is broken.

The thing that has kept me going is our life together, the community of the Holy Spirit that we share in this place, and the sense of God's presence among us. I am grateful for your kindness and gentleness with me and for the many signs of love and concern I have received.

I believe it is important in times of stress that we discover what is most important to us. In this time of trouble, when we so desperately need answers, what we have is each other, what we have is our common life. As imperfect as we are, we can still find love, joy, and peace, by God's grace, as we live and walk by the Spirit.

There will be a lot of sadness in us for a long time, for we have suffered a tremendous loss in our friend's death. We will continue to feel angry and even afraid sometimes because of the way he died and because of the circumstances that surrounded his death. But as God gives us hope, we can live and go forward, bringing our past, even this past, into a new day.

*J. Ellsworth Kalas* was senior minister of the Church of the Saviour (United Methodist) in Cleveland, Ohio, for sixteen years. Prior to that he was senior minister of the First United Methodist Church, Madison, Wisconsin, and at the First United Methodist Church in Green Bay, Wisconsin, following a pastorate in the Wesley and Concord churches in and near Watertown, Wisconsin. He graduated from the University of Wisconsin and Garrett-Evangelical Theological Seminary and did additional graduate study at the University of Wisconsin and Harvard University. His published books include *The Power of Believing* (Word) and *Reading the Signs* (CSS of Ohio).

This sermon was preached for the congregation at the Church of the Saviour and for a radio and cable television audience. Although Mr. Kalas had several times worked with families that had been devastated by suicide, he had never before dealt with the event in a Sunday morning sermon. His aim was to handle the subject in such a way that it would be helpful to people, whatever their present state of life, and would be a conveyer of hope rather than depression.

# 5

## Soul at the End
## of Its Rope

### Psalm 13

## J. Ellsworth Kalas

If you're very alert as you walk through the great old city
of Edinburgh, Scotland, you'll notice a tiny alleyway,
hardly wide enough for two persons to pass. Over it is the
carving of a boy's face, now much dimmed by years of
weather, and a message: "Heave away, chaps, I'm no' dead
yet."

The face and message are carved in honor of something
that happened long ago at that spot. An accident buried a
number of persons under the rubble of a fallen building.
For hours men struggled to dig through the bricks and dirt
to see if there were any survivors. At last they concluded
that their effort was hopeless, so they would give up their
search. At that point the Scottish lad summoned the energy
to call out his message: "Heave away, chaps, I'm no' dead
yet."

My memory often takes me back to that little alleyway
when I read another statistic or hear another individual
story about suicide. I ponder how desperately most of us,
most of the time, cling to life, how we will hold to it against
all odds. If we are physically ill, we push science and
physicians to the limit to extend life. Those who are on the
penitentiary's death row plead with lawyers and loved ones
to save their lives. Prisoners of war undergo unimaginable

torture and deprivation while they hold doggedly to the prospect of another day. How is it, when most of the time life is such a cherished commodity, that people by the tens of thousands choose violently to throw it away?

I'm very sure that some of you, at this moment, are withdrawing from what I'm saying. You don't want to hear a minister—or anyone else, for that matter—talk about suicide. Yet in looking back a while ago over virtually a lifetime of preaching, I realized that not only had I never preached on the subject, I'd never heard anyone else do so.

I was startled that this was so, and unnerved at my own omission. After all, suicide is not like flu or polio or even like cancer; it is something intimately related to our state of mind and to the struggles of the human soul. In a sense, it is an intensely religious subject, because it has to do with our attitude toward ourselves, God, and the value of human life. There could hardly be a subject more directly related to the trinity of faith, hope, and love, because when a person chooses suicide, he or she apparently feels that there is no reason for faith, no hope, and no one who loves.

In truth, suicide is a present and growing issue. On a typical day, seventy persons in America will take their own lives. That adds up to 26,000 persons a year. And of course that figure is low, because some people are successful in disguising their suicide so it is interpreted as an accident.

Who commits suicide? *Time* magazine reports that the highest suicide rate is among the elderly. Experts reason that this is a result of the depression that many older people feel. This problem of depression is accentuated by the amount and variety of prescription drugs the elderly use.[1]

But, ironically, suicide is also a major cause of death among the young—that is, for those between fifteen and twenty-four years of age. It is the third leading

---

[1] *Time,* February 22, 1988, p. 77.

cause of death for this age group. Six thousand young
people kill themselves each year, and 250,000 try to do
so.[2]

Incidentally, that latter figure is a significant one. It used
to be said that people who talk about taking their lives
never do so. Now we know better. Indeed, probably a
majority of those who attempt suicide give warning signals
by mentioning it to someone, as if hoping thus to elicit help.
And 12 percent of the people who attempt suicide unsuc-
cessfully will try it again within three months.

Sometimes we can understand why a person wants to
take his or her own life. Whether we approve of their escape
or not, we can understand their motivation. Many of us are
familiar with the name of Joni Eareckson, the young
woman who went swimming in Chesapeake Bay a few
weeks after graduating from high school, and in a freak
diving accident, ended up as a quadraplegic. She tells us
that at one point in the early period of her tragedy, she
wanted very much to take her own life, because it seemed to
her that there was nothing left to live for. She had been an
athletic, vigorous young woman; now she was doomed to
live in a bed or a wheelchair the rest of her life. The depth of
despair for her came in the realization that, as a quadraplegic, she couldn't even kill herself.

But what about people who attempt suicide when they
seem to have everything going for them? What about the
bright young athlete, the solid student, the successful
business or professional person? How is it that some people
try to take their own lives when the rest of us think they
have everything to live for?

Such instances remind us (and we've all known cases of
this kind) that we never really know what's going on in
another person's life or mind. The storm one person sails
through, bloody but unbowed, utterly destroys another.
When I was a boy, I overheard my parents talking with their
friends about a farmer who, in the dark year of 1932, took

---

[2] *World Book Year Book,* 1987, p. 248.

his life. They said that debts and crop failures simply drove him overboard. But other farmers weathered that storm. How come? I knew a man, in his sixties, who grieved over the death of his wife until finally he hanged himself. How come, when others survive as widows or widowers? I knew a man who took his life at a high point in his career, because he was being maligned by the press and bitterly attacked by the public. They said he just couldn't take any more abuse. How come he broke, while others survive similar abuse?

No one should venture easy answers to such questions. The questions are as complex as is the human psyche. And yet faith ought to have a word to say, a word spoken in gentleness and humility. Any word I might offer would surely have to be a humble word. On the one hand, I don't think I've ever considered suicide; it's almost completely foreign to my temperament and nature, so it's hard for me to get inside the skin of those who do consider it. But on the other hand, I've known times in my life when I had no real incentive to live and when, in truth, I was simply waiting for death to come. I wonder how many people live some of their days—perhaps many of them—in a kind of passive suicide? And how different, really, is the spirit of passive suicide from the deed that ends in tragedy?

There was a man long ago who had every reason to want to die. As the Bible reports his story, he lost his extensive fortune and shortly thereafter suffered the tragic death of his seven sons and three daughters. Soon his health broke too, and he was driven to the very end of his rope. His wife looked at his miserable, hopeless condition and said, "Why don't you curse God and die?" That is, Why not put an end to it all? Why go on?

But he hung on, and eventually he fought his way back. How did he do it? Two things strike me about this man, whose name was Job. He had great faith in God. From the pit of his private hell he cried, "I know that my Redeemer lives . . . ; from my flesh, I shall see

God" (Job 19:25–26). No matter how bad the circumstances, he kept his confidence in God. And he was sure, somehow, that he would someday see God on his side.

That's also the mood of the poet who wrote our scripture lesson of the morning, Psalm 13. This man—probably David, the shepherd king—was very candid with God. "Will you forget me forever?" he cried. "How long will you hide your face from me?" And yet, as he neared the very end of his rope, faith took over.

> But I have trusted in thy steadfast love;
> my heart shall rejoice in thy salvation.
> Psalm 13:5

Something deep in his soul was confident that God would not let him down. He was angry with God and despairing of his circumstances, yet he felt, in the pit of his being, that ultimately God would see him through.

It's so important to remember that God is on our side. There are times when we may think that everything else is against us. Our circumstances may not seem hopeless to others, but from where we sit it's as if we are emotional quadraplegics; we have no strength to grapple with life. At such times, we need to know something about the ultimate goodness of God.

When I was a young man, I was introduced to Frederick W. Faber's great hymn, "There's a Wideness in God's Mercy." It quickly became one of my favorites. Years later I learned that there are nine verses in the poem that don't appear in our hymnals. One of the omitted verses is especially worth repeating:

> But we make [God's] love too narrow
> By false limits of our own:
> And we magnify his strictness
> With a zeal he will not own.[3]

---

[3] Frederick Faber, quoted in Robert Guy McCutchan, *Our Hymnody,* p. 107.

In times of despair and self-doubt, it's so easy to put a mean face on God. Hell knows that if we lose the sense of God's friendship in the valley of the shadow, we've lost everything. We need therefore to develop, through the varying fortunes of life, a sound conviction that God is good and that his love is "broader than the measure of man's mind." And when some vagrant voice says, "Life is hopeless and God is against you," we can then rise up to say, "Don't try to fool me about God! I know his mercy, his loving-kindness. This is a ground where I will not be shaken."

The other thing that strikes me about Job is that he somehow held onto his own integrity. "Till I die," he said, "I will not put away my integrity from me" (Job 27:5b). He was confident that when the final showdown came, he would "come forth as gold." I find the same mood in many of the psalms. Ready as the psalmists were to confess their sins and to recognize their shortcomings, they also were quick to say, "I've done my best, and I think you will respect me for that, O Lord."

A fine seventeen-year-old took his life a few months ago in Colorado. In a note to his parents he said, "I am a terrible son, I haven't been able to communicate with you, although you have tried. . . . I was not doing anything right in school, in swimming or socially."[4] In truth, he was almost a model kid, who testified to being a born-again Christian. But all of us have times when we look down on ourselves, and hell is always ready to assist that mood. After all, the very word "Satan" means adversary or accuser. On a day when we feel rejected, unsuccessful, unworthy, the adversary is quick to chide and torment us. At such a time we need a strong sense of our worth before God. Something in us must be ready to say, "I may not be perfect, but I'm made of awfully good stuff, because I'm made in God's image; and I'm made well, because I came from the hand of the Great Designer."

---

[4] *USA Today,* Nov. 11, 1987, pp. 1–2.

In this sermon I've used the figure of speech of a soul at the end of its rope. It occurs to me that over the years I've heard two apparently conflicting lines of advice as to what one should do when at the end of the rope. Someone once told me, "When you get to the end of your rope, tie a knot and hang on for dear life." But another person said, "When you get to the end of your rope, just let go—and you'll discover that underneath are the everlasting arms of God."

From Job and the psalmists I've concluded that both lines of advice are right. On the one hand, we need to take new courage in our own integrity and worth; on the other, we must cast ourselves more surely than ever on the mercy and love of God. But in either instance, know that the "end of your rope" is not really a hopeless place. Not when there is God, and not when God has invested in us such infinite quality.

Suicide is not a new phenomenon. It is probably as old as the human race; after all, there are seven suicides recorded in the Bible. But its power is perhaps greater in our rather hectic, impersonal times. We need therefore to build a faith to cope with it—in our own lives, and in those friends or acquaintances who are somewhere near the end of their rope. We need to know, beyond any shadow of doubt, that God is good and is on our side; and that we are made well and are worth saving. We need to know that at the heart of this universe stand grace and love. Thanks be to God. Amen.

*Janis J. Kinens* was born in Bruckberg, West Germany, and came to the United States at age five. He lived in Kalamazoo, Michigan, and later studied at Western Michigan University and the Cleveland Art Institute. After military service in Vietnam, he completed his undergraduate degree with a major in art. Following a brief teaching career, he attended the Lutheran School of Theology in Chicago, from which he holds the Doctor of Ministry degree. He is now pastor of the Pentecost Evangelical Lutheran Church in Milwaukee, Wisconsin.

After the suicide of an active, intelligent, and popular young man had sent shock waves through his congregation, Dr. Kinens was faced, for the first time, with having to deal directly with the grief and guilt that followed. This sermon was preached at a memorial service for the young man.

# 6

## What Is Lost
## Shall Be Found

*2 Samuel 12:15–23; John 14:1–11*

### Janis J. Kinens

*What is lost shall be found, though not always in the same
place.*

His life began and ends at the baptismal font. Life for you
and me began at the baptismal font, and one day it will end
there as certainly as you hear my words at this moment.
These things are certainties. The rest is a mystery, and we
do not understand it.

You and I have, these last few days, tried to figure out just
what happened to him. We have spoken endless hours. We
have cried, worried, become angry. We have shouted in
disbelief and screamed at the unfairness of it all. We have
even blamed him and, whether acknowledged or not, we
have blamed God.

And perhaps one of the reasons why we have received so
little comfort from these things is that they are very
misplaced. Our Christian gospel tells us that judgment and
blame belong to God, not us—and yet we so delight in
it!

Perhaps in death, he will be able to teach us what he
could not in life. He tried desperately to do it, but for the
most part we did not seem to listen to him.

In the bulletin you will find words that he wrote less than a year ago, just after Easter. These are deep and profound words. These are words of hope in the midst of despair: "What is lost shall be found, though not always in the same place."

We have lost him in a sense, but in another sense he will always be with us. This is the Christian message that we receive in that splash of water we call baptism. It is the resurrection message that Jesus tried to get his disciples to understand and, failing that, showed them by his own death and resurrection.

He made many wonderful choices in life. He was a gifted thinker and writer. He was a talented swimmer, played soccer, was very physical, yet had the power of concentration and intellect to play a challenging game of chess.

He made many wonderful choices in life, but tragically, for complex reasons that will remain a mystery to us, he made one very wrong choice. For reasons beyond our understanding, he thought death would offer him something that life did not. This was a horrible mistake, and because of this one very wrong choice, we who are left have lost a very precious presence and talent from our lives.

To put it bluntly and truthfully, it is such a waste! You see, all of the universe unfolds toward life, struggles to live and to be. It is a process that surrounds and enfolds us.

Ironically, he wrote about that in an essay, "The Fires of Creation." After describing the process of rock and earth formation through the fires of creation, he wrote:

> Without the fires in the sky and the warmth they provide they will lose the power to be different from the others. They will lose their life. For now they join, becoming no longer just a small collection. They are joining, becoming larger and larger in their pieces. Unlike the lifeless rocks that surround them, they grow into larger pieces instead of breaking down into smaller and smaller pieces.

To choose death over life negates the very forces of creation and the will of God for creation! And although he could articulate that process in words, for reasons unknown to us the truth had not found a place in his heart.

And what a heart he had! He was able to love with an intensity and write about it with eloquence. In his journal entry dated April 1986, he wrote:

> She stands all alone looking solemn and forgotten. Her face breaks into a beautiful smile . . . more beautiful than diamonds or gold. . . . I see a beautiful love, one who no matter how she is attacked can never, ever be broken. I think this is the one whom I love. I cannot sleep, for her face keeps me awake. I cannot look, for she is all I see. My mind doesn't work, for she uses its every power. Yet why I cannot speak to her is for fear. Her dark eyes, her blond hair, her beautiful smile, all seem to isolate her. Maybe I am mad for trying to love one such as this. I cannot but see through tainted eyes.

And this, of course, is part of the great tragedy of his death, that he saw most everything through tainted eyes, eyes tainted by loneliness, fear of rejection, family discord, lack of stability, insecurity, low self-esteem—and so he made the wrong choice! Whether these were, in fact, true matters very little, for he saw and experienced life through these eyes and believed it was so. And he made the wrong choice!

Though tainted, his vision had a clarity to it, as we see from his observation of life around him. In a journal entry of May 1986 he wrote:

> I see people running like ants, each doing what he or she does, believing their own beliefs, and having their own morals. . . . It's so funny . . . but sad. . . . If I become great and important, will I scorn others as they have scorned me?

It is as if he could not fully accept the fact that there were so many of us who did respect and love him, who did appreciate his impish smile and playful presence, who were at times awed by the depth of his character and sensitivity.

And yet it is so hard to celebrate the gifts he had when we stand in the presence of such unnecessary waste.

The great flaw we see here is one that is as old as the history of humankind: that death is somehow a friend. It is not! The entire gospel message stands or falls on the belief that death is the enemy. It is death that separates us from those we love, it is death that ceases our movements and play, death that brings darkness into our lives and loneliness into our hearts. Of course, death is a reality. It happens every day, all around us, and one day it will happen to us as well, but what death is not is an option. There are optional life-styles, optional belief systems, optional attitudes, optional understandings of all things, but never is death an option for those who love life. That is why Paul said the strong words, "Death is the last enemy to be destroyed" (1 Cor. 15:26).

And yet Paul also said, "Death, where is thy victory? Death, where is thy sting?" (1 Cor. 15:55). Paul was reminding us that death does not have the last word. And in this case it does not have the last word. You are a living witness to that. Through his baptism, he was given the keys to eternal life, was touched and marked by Jesus Christ in a covenant that is everlasting and, especially in the midst of death, speaks to us of life.

Many of you, with your love, spoke to him about life. In his journal he wrote, "Today we start a canoe trip. Too bad_____and_____couldn't come. Either or both would make it much more interesting. But I'll still enjoy the company of my adopted family—my Explorer post!" Friends figured in his life in many important ways. You should know how much light you brought into his loneliness. Any of you who showed interest in his life gave him hope, as well. The smallest kindness or notice was received with gratitude. Again, an entry from his journal: "_____asked me if I would join him outside while he had a smoke. Though I may never receive another invitation from him, I know he considers me a friend and will help me if I need it."

Where do we go from here? What should we feel and say?

There are three basic or classic responses that people have to death. Two of them lead to a dead end. The third, difficult as it is, can bring us to healing.

The first response, and probably the worst, is also most common. We all, well-meaning Christians and friends, will say things like, "Oh, it was God's will. God wanted him in heaven. That's just the way it was meant to be," and so on, as if we should be grateful to have been visited by God in all of this. This is a very bad response to the death of anyone. Who are we to think that we can speak in God's place and tell others what God desires for their lives? When we do, especially those of us who are charged with that awesome responsibility, we will find throughout the gospel that God wants us to live, to be whole people, to enjoy life, and to be graced with love. God does not will us destruction, death, and waste. So please don't put words in God's mouth. It will bring very little comfort to this family or any other.

The second response is a bit more responsible, actually needed, especially when something like this happens. It is the logical or analytical response, very common to us all. In this response, we begin by asking questions. Why? Why did he do this? What did I say or do wrong to bring it about? Did someone pressure him? Where was I when he needed me? What could I have said or done to prevent this? I wonder why? Why? Why? Through our analysis, we may even reach a conclusion. Perhaps it was a chemical imbalance; perhaps the peer pressure was too great; perhaps parents figured into it in ways they do not understand. Perhaps, perhaps, perhaps.

And even when we can draw a conclusion, a picture of what happened and why, we have done very little about the heartache and emptiness that results when we lose someone we love. To heal those, we need yet a third response to death. It is the one we heard about in the Old Testament lesson about King David.

You see, when King David felt he could do something about the health of his son, he was very involved, very concerned, as he should have been. But when the boy died, he knew it was beyond his reach to do anything, so he got up, washed, and went to the temple to pray. He went to church! He began to live again! He knew he could not bring his son back to life, even though he himself would someday die. This third way of reacting to death is the one I pray you will all take. This third way is called forgiveness. We begin by forgiving, forgiving ourselves, forgiving the people we do not like, forgiving God, forgiving him, forgiving circumstances. If you can begin to do this, you will begin to heal. Cast the blame, the need for blame, aside, and live again.

As long as we allow the bitterness of blame to enslave us, we cannot truly live. The only hope we have is forgiveness. If we can learn to do that, we can also celebrate the gifts he shared with us in his short life. We can even believe the baptismal promise that is his and yours and mine, the promise that through Jesus Christ the victory has been won, and even the senseless and wrongheaded decision that has brought us all together this evening cannot begin to wipe it out!

> What is lost shall be found, though not always in the same place.

*A. Morgan Parker* is a retired U.S. Navy chaplain, now pastor of the San Luis Rey Valley United Methodist Church in California. While stationed near Washington, D.C., he earned the Doctor of Ministry degree at Wesley Theological Seminary. His project thesis was later published as *Suicide Among Young Adults.*

When one of the members of the congregation lost her older brother from a self-inflicted gunshot wound, Dr. Parker realized the high degree of community awareness and concern about suicide. Fifty percent of the members of the congregation were retirees, a high-risk group for suicide. He preached the sermon to reduce anxiety stemming from the mystery surrounding suicidal behavior and to offer assurance that a caring, compassionate response can make a vital difference.

# 7

# Hearing the Cry

## A. Morgan Parker

We have just come through the really great and joyous seasons of Easter, the chartering of our new church, the grandeur of Mother's Day, the celebration of the Christian home and family. Now we turn, rather abruptly, from that to another side of the story, to what I call the "saddest season," a season that spans, if you can believe it, this same season of great joy, this springtime. I take up, as others have requested I do, an area in which my own studies have led to the publication of a book, as well as journal and magazine articles. This is the very tragic and ever-timely subject of suicide.

We want to look this morning at its dynamics, its occurrences, its possible prevention, and the particular resources that Christian faith brings to this area of crisis. And crisis is, indeed, the word for it.

You've been reading articles and hearing news releases about suicides recently, particularly suicides by teenagers and young people in automobiles, even in groups. You've heard about mass suicide in various states and around the world, where people have resorted to this greatest of human tragedies.

My own study focused on young adults, primarily in the armed services, but also across our culture. It is among youth and young adults that we have seen the most dramatic increase in suicide rates in the last two decades in our society. We as Christians should particularly understand and feel ourselves prepared and ready to respond to this great crisis.

Whenever we hear about such problems in our midst, in our community, in our families, there is always an enormous amount of shock and surprise, along with trauma and heartache. A great mystery envelops us as we exclaim, "How on earth could this have happened to Jack [or Sue]? He [or she] was the strongest, most secure, stable person. I'm shocked and surprised!"

Suicide always comes to us as something that seems incomprehensible, beyond our grasping. Yet those persons who have given themselves to lifelong research and study of the subject tell us that, in an amazing way, suicide is quite predictable. Once we are aware of some basic factors, we can become instruments of prevention and healing.

The first basic we need to understand is that there is a season for suicide. It comes between about the fifteenth of March and the fifteenth of May. Suicides happen more often in the springtime of the year than at any other time.

Researchers tell us that apparently while the rest of the world is blossoming and looking great, some people cannot stand the contrast with their own heartache and grief. They had been able to manage in midwinter when everything else was dreary.

Through all sorts of holiday seasons—Christmas, New Year's—suicide rates go up for the same reason. We need to be sensitive at those times, when the "cry for help" described by Shneidman and Farberow in their book *Clues to Suicide* is most pronounced.

We can learn some very basic things about suicide from workers at suicide prevention centers. I've had the privilege of working with some of the 135 centers from Los Angeles to Boston. Volunteers staff the phones 24 hours a day, seven days a week. They have in front of them lethality rating scales. When a person calls, the criteria listed on these scales are checked. First of all, they ask if the caller is male or female, although they will probably know that from the voice. They are interested because three or four times as many men as women take their lives in this country. The other side of the story is that three or four times as many women as men attempt suicide. An interesting parallel to these factors is that the actual act of suicide is more likely to take place midweek, the highest point of the week being Thursday. However, suicide attempts come more often on weekends, in spare time when people are not as active. Thus women may call on the weekend, threatening to use pills, razor blades, or gas. But men who call during the week are more likely actually to use their guns, knives, ropes, or other lethal implements.

So first of all the phone counselor wants to know whether the caller is a man or woman, and understands a great deal from the answer. The counselor next wants to know the ethnic and racial background, because in this country whites take their own lives far more often than any other group.

The third thing interviewers ask is the religious preference. In this country, Protestants take their own lives seven times more often than Roman Catholics. We Protestants have a history of doing our own thing. Whatever our conscience tells us is correct is fine. The other side of the Christian family, the Roman Catholic tradition, teaches its members to listen to the person in authority. The history and tradition of the church provide a strong social support system. But we Protestants are lone, independent, self-made persons who go out not only to follow our own course but finally to do ourselves in.

This characteristic holds true around the world as you look at the ratings. The Protestant countries are high, the Catholic countries are low. In the Hispanic countries to the south of us, the suicide rate is four or five per hundred thousand. However, in Scandinavia the rate is thirty to thirty-five per hundred thousand.

You can imagine my dismay as a doctoral student when I started this research and went to the National Institutes of

Health to ask about some studies. They said, "Wouldn't you know it—you are a prime candidate for suicide! A white male Protestant in graduate school, struggling with intense pressure to do well." All I had to do was say that I was thinking about suicide and I would have had people rush to render aid. That is what happens if you say over the phone, "I'm thinking about it . . . I'm talking suicide," and you meet these criteria. You will have enough points to keep the counselor on the line.

There are other things the counselor would want to know: Have you been ill or hospitalized in the last six months? Are you living alone? Have you experienced a deep personal loss in your family? Have you attempted suicide before? Some figures say that as high as 10 percent of those who actually commit suicide have previously tried. Have you actually put something in writing in the form of a suicide note? A much higher rating is given for that. And have you chosen a method? How would you do this thing? If you are going to take your life, and you say, "I have the forty-five in my hand—I am going to use it—I've got the shells here," they will keep you on the line until the police, the pastor, or someone can be with you and bring immediate help.

These are predictable, understandable things. They clear up the mystery about suicidal behavior. We know the time of year to be most sensitive. We know the time of week; we even know the time of day because we are told it is in the most active time, during working hours, that people are more likely to take their own lives. We can see on charts that people do not die during lunch hour or coffee breaks. We know a great deal, then, about the dynamics affecting the person who talks about suicide.

We are also interested in knowing what the Bible has to show us about this phenomenon. Two key examples come from scripture. One is King Saul of the Old Testament. In defeat and loss of battle, the king of Israel takes his own life upon Mount Gilboa with the words echoing out of scripture, "How the mighty have fallen." And great grief, as you can imagine, fell across the land. But there's no real word of condemnation for what the king did.

In the New Testament, the classic figure is Judas Iscariot. We know the agony, the heartache of all that was about him in his betrayal, and how he went out to hang himself. Again, there is no great ridicule or condemnation for the form of death. Isn't it interesting, then, how the church has adopted a very strong stance against suicide, which accounts for the strong Catholic position against suicide today? All through history, theologians have said suicide is a mortal sin, it's an act against God. You do not belong to yourself, you belong to God. You do not have the right to take your own life. Suicide was generally against the law. In the Middle Ages, your body would be taken out to the edge of town, a stake would be driven through it, and you would be left there on the crossroads. Your family's property would be confiscated, and you would not be buried in the consecrated cemetery. There was great punishment, if you broke the law of the church and of the land!

While suicide is contrary to the law in certain places and circumstances today, survivors are rarely punished. However, in a majority of states, assisting in a suicide is prosecuted as either murder or first-degree manslaughter. Both legal and biomedical ethical questions relating to suicidal acts are currently pressing for insight and decision.

Today we still have strong convictions against suicide, as stated in a variety of theological writings, but we also have a far more compassionate understanding of the individual involved. Not only do we empathize with the pain, suffering, and tragedy one may have endured, but we also see the possibility of "investing" oneself in a distinct way. Remember Jesus' words of John 15:13, "Greater love has no man than this, that a man lay down his life for his friends." Some extreme acts of sacrificial heroism, as in giving one's life jacket to a child or an injured survivor, may follow even in the footsteps of Jesus. Theologians like Dietrich Bonhoeffer have helped us to understand and accept this rare and exalted self-giving.

In any case, we in the Christian tradition understand the infinite forgiveness and mercy of Almighty God. We understand God's love to all peoples and we should be like the Befrienders who answer phone lines around the world, saying, "Somebody cares, somebody loves you." We too want to listen to their story, hear their problems, and respond to them in any compassionate, supportive, encouraging way we can. That alone, we know from all the research, saves lives. The average listening time is twenty minutes. If you can give twenty minutes to someone who says, "I think I am going to kill myself," you can save the person's life. By just responding, "Why in the world? What is going on with you? What are you feeling? Tell me about it," you can stop people from taking their lives. The problem is, too many have responded, "Oh, you're just kidding! You wouldn't do a thing like that! Sorry, I have to get back to work, coffee break is over, I have no time for this nonsense." Then people take their lives. The sensitive, understanding, supportive people of the world will save lives.

When we've done psychological autopsies after death, we discover there were clues given every day, every month, in families or among friends telling people, both overtly and implicitly that the person was thinking of taking his or her life. People have said, "I'm canceling all subscriptions, giving up all memberships. I won't need this organization anymore." No one said, "Why? Why?" The clues were strong and clear. Christians are those above all who should say, "We care. What's going on with you? Let's talk about it." If this happens, invariably the individual comes to a better answer. There's a better way of dealing with trauma, crisis, or loss than to lay one's life down needlessly. When one is in the midst of a careless society, a careless community, one could be so obsessed and pent up emotionally that one might go out and do this thing. If one gets to the phone line, to the counselor, to the police, or to a friend, and talks it out, things are different and changed. Lives are saved.

Sometimes the tragedy has already occurred. What we are able to say seems insufficient, but we are often the ones who are called to minister to the survivors. We want to remember 2 Corinthians 5:1, which says there is an eternal home for all of us when we are gone. And our God is forgiving. God is compassionate and accepting of us in our tragedies. God keeps us and holds us closely. We want to remember to share with survivors the words from Romans 8:38–39, that there is absolutely nothing that can separate us from the love of God! God is love and loves us in every crisis.

John 10:10 reminds us again of Jesus' words, "I came that they may have life, and have it abundantly." That's the bottom line. Jesus has come for that. He has commissioned us for that and reminded us of it and sent us to be his ambassadors—to give the word of life, the word of hope, the word of encouragement to those in darkness, to say there is another way, there is someone who cares. He sends us to say, "I care enough to be with you, and together we go to God, who will save us, redeem us, and renew us always."

We are God's people now and forever in light or darkness, joy or woe. And together we thank and praise our God for everlasting life.

**William E. Phipps** is a Professor of Religion and Philosophy at Davis and Elkins College in Elkins, West Virginia. His book, *Death: Confronting the Reality,* was published by John Knox Press in 1987. *Cremation Concerns* was published by Thomas Books in 1989.

For fifteen years he has taught a death education course which includes a unit on suicide. Year after year, the subject of suicide is chosen as a special research topic more than any other on the list of suggested topics. Dr. Phipps believes this desire to probe the subject reflects a lack of consideration of it in the homes, schools, and churches from which the students have come. This sermon was motivated by a recognition that the issue needs to be brought out of the closet and into the light, off campus as well as on.

# 8

# Is Suicide Ever
# a Christian's Right?

## William E. Phipps

Our hymns at this service—"God Moves in a Mysterious Way," "O for a Closer Walk with God," and "Sometimes a Light Surprises"—were all composed by a person who had a long struggle with impulses to kill himself. William Cowper first attempted suicide when he was a young English lawyer. During a fit of madness, he tried to penetrate his heart with a penknife, but the point was broken. He then resorted to hanging himself with a garter, but it slipped off the nail. After eighteen months in a "lunatic asylum," he was released and became a friend of John Newton, the famous evangelical minister. Knowing Cowper's poetic abilities, Newton suggested that they jointly publish a hymnbook. "Amazing Grace" became Newton's most famous contribution, and "God Moves in a Mysterious Way" became Cowper's best-known hymn. That majestic hymn was written after he went through the horror of another mental breakdown. At that time he felt God demanded that he kill himself, like Judas, in order to hasten his final doom in hell. But he then rose out of the valley of the dark shadow to enjoy decades as the most popular poet of his eighteenth-century era. Even so, he ended his life in a mental institution, where he wrote his famous poem of despair, "The Castaway." Would we think differently of Cowper if he had succeeded in committing suicide?

Over the centuries, attempted or accomplished suicide has seldom been discussed either outside or inside the church. In the United States, a person is more likely to kill himself or herself than to be killed by someone else. This fact is rarely recognized, because newspapers make headlines of homicides but they report few suicides. Lately the media have been giving attention to the alarming rate of youth suicide. But now, as in the past, the older generation accounts for the highest suicide rate. The rate of male suicides is several times that of females, and the rate among whites is double that among blacks. You are looking at one who belongs to the highest risk group—an older white male Protestant professional!

Suicide remains a taboo subject, even though there are about as many suicides in the nation each year as there were American deaths in the entire Vietnam War. Of these 50,000 annual suicide deaths, about half are not reported as such on death certificates. Even though suicide occurs frequently in virtually every community, I have never heard or read a sermon on the subject. No mention is made of suicide in the several books I possess on Christian moral problems.

What guidance does the Bible and church history give on suicide? The Bible tells of seven self-killings (Judg. 9:54; 16:30; 1 Sam. 31:4; 31:5; 2 Sam. 17:23; 1 Kings 16:18; Matt. 27:5).The best known is that of betrayer Judas. A thousand years earlier, King Saul fell on his sword rather than become a captive of the Philistines who had defeated his army. Samson, another notable suicide, desired to take revenge on the Philistines who had tortured him. He was willing to die in the temple that he was collapsing on his enemies. Significantly, the biblical writers neither condemn nor commend those whom they record as having taken their own lives. Perhaps the narrators thought it was fitting for Samson, Saul, and Judas to respond to their varied situations by committing suicide.

In early Christianity, suicide was sometimes regarded as a virtuous act. Eusebius, in his account of martyrs at Antioch, tells of a mother who taught her two beautiful unmarried daughters to regard rape as the most dreadful thing that could happen to them. Eventually the mother and daughters were captured by a band of lustful soldiers. On realizing their plight, they modestly requested to be excused for a minute. They then threw themselves into a nearby river and drowned.

In the fourth century, Bishop Augustine discussed suicides at length. Recognizing that certain Christian women had committed suicide rather than permit their bodies to be ravaged, Augustine granted that they *may* have done what was right in the sight of God. But, in his view, the women should not have assumed that rape would necessarily deprive them of their purity. Purity is a state of mind, he affirmed, so bodily violence cannot damage it. Job kept his moral integrity amid terrible suffering and did not take his life, Augustine noted. He found it significant that at no point does the Bible make it lawful to take one's own life. The command "Thou shalt not kill" implies, he argued, that one's own life, as well as the lives of others, should be preserved. Samson's suicide was a rare exception to this rule, for he received special divine permission. Concluded Augustine, "He who knows it is unlawful to kill himself may nevertheless do so if he is ordered by God."[1]

Augustine's viewpoint on suicide has heavily influenced all Christians. Thomas Aquinas, the most outstanding of Roman Catholic theologians, argued that suicide is a sin against self, neighbor, and God. First, suicide is contrary to nature; every living organism naturally desires to preserve its life. Second, it is contrary to our social obligations; the whole human community is injured by self-killing. Third, suicide is contrary to our religious rights; God alone should decide when a person will live or die. Aquinas reasoned, "To bring death upon oneself in order to escape the other

---

[1] *The City of God,* book 1, sections 18–26.

afflictions of this life is to adopt a greater evil in order to avoid a lesser. . . . Suicide is the most fatal of sins because it cannot be repented of."[2] The poet Dante, following Aquinas's theology, placed those who take their own lives on the seventh level of hell, below the greedy and the murderous. For centuries, those who committed the unconfessed and therefore unforgivable sin of suicide were not buried in cemeteries that Catholic priests had consecrated.

In 1608 John Donne wrote a treatise in which he agreed with Augustine that even though suicide is generally a "damnable wickedness," it is nevertheless permissible if commanded by God. He was the first Englishman and one of the few Christians ever to argue that suicide could in exceptional cases be a "summons from God." Donne believed that the voice of God was transmitted to humans through conscientious reasoning, especially about matters on which the Bible gives no definite judgment.

Most Christians and non-Christians today will probably agree that Aquinas's condemnation of all suicides is too harsh. There is no basis for regarding suicide as the most deadly sin. As we have seen, there is no explicit prohibition of suicide anywhere in the Bible. This reflection on Judeo-Christian tradition provides some guidance for facing current dilemmas. Modern medicine occasionally extends artificially the time of death—a fact that has generated fresh inquiry into situations in which suicide might be acceptable.

Consider the case of an elderly man who was found to have an erratic heartbeat, an enlarged prostate, a bowel obstruction, and arthritic joints when admitted to a hospital. On learning that surgery was being planned, he pleaded,

> Listen, doctor, I don't want to die with tubes sticking out all over me. I don't want my children to remember their father that way. I'm old and tired and have seen enough of life,

---

[2] *Summa Theologica* 2-2, questions 64–65.

believe me. But still I want to be a man, not a vegetable that someone comes and waters every day. You see, the engine is broken down; it is time for the engineer to abandon it.

Despite this eloquent request, a tube for feeding was placed down the old man's nose into his stomach. Intravenous injections were made four times a day. Later the man was hooked up to a respirator to increase his oxygen intake. One night he reached over and switched off his respirator. For several hours the hospital staff did not realize what had happened. On the bedside they found this suicide note: "Death is not the enemy, doctor. Inhumanity is." The plight of this gentleman illustrates why many of the elderly dread hospitalization, not death.

Consider also the much-publicized death of Elizabeth and Henry Pitney Van Dusen. Pitney, age seventy-seven, was the former president of New York's Union Theological Seminary and a distinguished Presbyterian minister. He and his wife, Elizabeth, age eighty, discussed suicide with their family and friends and then signed a pact before taking an overdose of sleeping pills. She wrote:

> We have both had full and satisfying lives. . . . But since Pitney had his stroke five years ago, we have not been able to do any of the things we want to do . . . and my arthritis is much worse. There are too many helpless old people who without modern medicinal care would have died, and we feel God would have allowed them to die when their time came. Nowadays it is difficult to die. We feel that this way we are taking will become more usual and acceptable as the years pass. . . . We are both increasingly weak and unwell, and who would want to die in a nursing home? . . . "O Lamb of God that takest away the sins of the world, grant us thy peace."[3]

In 1980 a group of psychiatrists, philosophers, and theologians prepared a statement on suicide for the terminally ill which is relevant to these cases. It reads:

---

[3] Linnea Pearson, with Ruth Purtilo, *Separate Paths,* pp. 134–135.

Historically, suicide has been judged as "sinful" by organized religion. . . . We do not dispute the contention that the majority of suicides represent a rejection of the "gift of life" and, as such, are evidence of severe emotional distress. We believe, however, that a person with a progressive terminal disease faces a unique situation—one which calls for a new look at traditional assumptions about the motivation for choosing suicide. In our view, this choice might be found to be reasoned, appropriate, altruistic, sacrificial, and loving. We can imagine that an individual faced with a debilitating, irreversible illness, who would have to endure intractable pain, mutilating surgery, or demeaning treatments—with added concern for the burden being placed on family and friends—might conclude that suicide was a reasonable, even generous, resolution to a process already moving inexorably toward death.[4]

In spite of the usual debilitating impact of suicide on survivors, we must ask, Are there any situations in which it is morally right? John Donne's position is a helpful guide for facing the broad range of circumstances confronting the Christian. There may be situations in which suicide can be a conscientious act resulting from a careful weighing of alternatives. The Van Dusens' suicide note, for example, displays serious and rational decision-making. After the couple died, a committee of the Presbytery of New York wisely concluded that "for some Christians, as a last resort in the gravest of situations, suicide may be an act of their Christian conscience."

---

[4] "Suicide: Is It an Acceptable Alternative for the Terminally Ill?" *Concern for Dying Newsletter,* Fall 1981, p. 4.

*Christine M. Smith* is Assistant Professor of Homiletics at Princeton Theological Seminary. She received the Ph.D. from the Graduate Theological Union in Berkeley, where she specialized in Liturgy and Proclamation. Earlier she had earned one degree at Ohio University in Athens, Ohio, and two degrees at The Methodist Theological School in Ohio.

This sermon is designed to enable a religious community to reflect theologically on God's redemptive activity in the midst of suicide. It is not intended to be a sermon that responds to a specific experience of suicide or to a particular context but is designed to aid the community in reflecting honestly on a complex and serious human issue. It attempts to call forth a faithful response from God's people to a profoundly mysterious human act.

# 9

# Embracing the Windstorm

## Christine M. Smith

Bless Yahweh, my soul,
Yahweh, my God, how great you are!
Clothed in majesty and splendour,
wearing the light as a robe!

You stretch out the heavens like a tent,
build your palace on the waters above,
making the clouds your chariot,
gliding on the wings of the wind,
appointing the winds your messengers,
flames of fire your servants.

You fixed the earth on its foundations,
for ever and ever it shall not be shaken. . . .

In the ravines you opened up springs
running down between the mountains,
supplying water for all the wild beasts;
the wild asses quench their thirst,
on their banks the birds of the air make their nests,
they sing among the leaves.

From your high halls you water the mountains,
satisfying the earth with the fruit of your works.
Psalm 104:1–5, 10–13, NJB

Elisabeth Kübler-Ross, in one of her books on death and dying, speaks about the power of embracing our greatest fears and the sculpturing marks that death leaves upon our lives:

> To love means never to be afraid of the windstorms of life: Should you shield the canyons from the windstorms you would never see the true beauty of their carvings. I hope this book encourages people to expose themselves to these windstorms, so that at the end of their own days, they will be proud to look in the mirror and be pleased with the carvings of their own canyon.[1]

When anyone in the human family takes her or his own life, we are left with a deafening windstorm. The multitude of emotions that sweep through our hearts and spirits are fierce and brutal at one moment and hauntingly sad at another. If we are distanced bystanders, the windstorm only holds us for a moment and then flings us quickly back into life. If we are those most lovingly connected, the windstorm will leave us forever changed. The wind of this death will begin the long and painful process of carving its way into the canyon walls of our souls. Whether one is held in the windstorm for only a moment or plunged into it for a long time, it leaves a permanent mark of transformation. Suicide is one of life's most overwhelming storms. It is mysterious beyond all our analyzing, all our searching, and all our naming. In the face of its profound message, we stand utterly vulnerable before each other and God.

The psalmist knows in an intimate way these mysterious moments of life. The faithful writer of Psalm 104 knows well the calming moments of created goodness, as well as the windstorms of life and faith, and boldly declares God's presence in the midst of all.

> You fixed the earth on its foundations,
> for ever and ever it shall not be shaken. . . .

---

[1] *To Live Until We Say Good-bye,* p. 155.

> In the ravines you opened up springs
> running down between the mountains,
> supplying water for all the wild beasts. . . .
>
> From your high halls you water the mountains,
> satisfying the earth with the fruit of your works.
> Psalm 104:5, 10–11, 13, NJB

Yet in strangely contrasting images, when compared to the pastoral scenes of peace and harmony, the psalmist quietly proclaims: "appointing the winds your messengers, flames of fire your servants." Surely God's people throughout time have known God's movement in swift transforming fire and God's presence in fierce swirling wind. Sometimes fire will serve us an unknown gift, and the wind, even though a storm, will carry a message.

Suicide is shocking! We are a people who want to forget that the threads of life and death are tied at every turn, part of the same fabric, woven into the very cloth of existence. And each time we forget, death shocks us as some intruder or enemy of life. We feel in these moments that death has taken hold of us against our will. We cannot fathom any human being willfully taking hold of death. But in reality this is what happens, and their numbers increase each year, in each generation. In the face of such a message, such an act, such a choice, where is the God the psalmist praises, the creator and sustainer of all we know? Where is God's redemptive power and presence?

I have little to say about God's activity in the contemplation and taking of one's own life. It is a mystery I am content to leave an ultimate mystery, but I do know something about what that action does to the rest of the human community. When suicide happens, we all must speak about some of the profound questions raised, the faithful responses made, and the affirmations of faith that are renewed. We need not look outside ourselves for God's redemptive activity; rather, in the face of suicide we are called to look within us and around us to see and feel how redemption is manifest among us. For those of us who do not shield ourselves, this event leaves carvings on the canyon walls of each of us that take on a peculiar beauty and hope.

If we are able to move beyond the "whys that we will never be able to answer," let go of the "what ifs that we will never be able to know," and set free the "if onlys" that keep us locked in the past, we will clear our minds and hearts to perceive and ask the larger questions of our own lives and life itself.

In a culture where life expectations continue to be extended, and where technology makes surviving more a reality at times than living, there are deep and complex responses to intentional suicide. A special older friend and I talk often about death, and about our mutual commitment to quality of life. Listening to her speak, I am often struck by the clarity of her thought and will regarding her own dying. She desires to live as long as life remains vital and her contributions to it meaningful, and when either of those possibilities cease to be, she hopes death will come quickly. I hear her deepest longing and often ponder how horrible it would be if she was ever forced to survive against her wishes. I can't help but wonder if most of us don't secretly celebrate the intentionality and clarity of those among us who will, and do, choose their own death when life is ultimately over.

In this country, the covenantal suicide of Elizabeth and Henry Pitney Van Dusen over a decade ago brought into our consciousness in a powerful way what choosing one's own death might mean. In their suicide letter, the Van Dusens expressed these feelings and affirmations:

> To all friends and relations. We hope that you will understand what we have done even though some of you will disapprove of it and be disillusioned by it. We have both had very full and satisfying lives. . . . Nowadays it is difficult to die. We feel that this way we are taking will become more usual and acceptable as the years pass. . . .We are not afraid to die.[2]

---

[2] Linnea Pearson, with Ruth Purtilo, *Separate Paths,* pp. 134–135.

It must be a liberating moment when one comes to know deep within one's spirit and heart that one is ready and able to let go of life as we know it, to embrace the living mystery that remains unknown. The wind of this intentionality, this clarity of thought and action, is redemptive for all of us. In a strange and profound way it calms the storm of meaninglessness and reclaims the promises of quality of life intended by our Creator for all creation.

In sharp contrast to this intentional act, how are we to respond when a fifteen-year-old boy walks slowly and silently behind a school building and shoots himself? How are we to cope when a brother hangs himself or a mother overdoses on too many pills? These moments feel like such an assault on life, we are paralyzed with grief. If God's redemptive activity is present and alive within these human horrors, we have a difficult time discerning it. God seems cruel in silence, powerless in the finality. If redemptive activity is only understood by us as God's capacity to control human choices, or our Creator's willingness miraculously to restore to life that which is dead, then God is painfully absent. Yet if redemptive activity involves bringing forth life from death, rebirth from letting go, and canyons of depth from terrorizing storms, then God is very much at work. Don't most of us ask deeper questions from life in the face of deaths that seem so lonely and despairing? In the Christian community we must all ask ourselves where we have failed to nurture and sustain life for each other, and where the power of death has strangled the fire of life in the deepest recesses of our own being. The psalmist speaks God's praises and sings unceasingly the steadfastness of life's goodness, yet on another day a lament will pour forth from this same person's heart. "Yahweh, my God, I call for help all day; I cry out to you all night. May my prayer come to you. Hear my cries for help, for my soul is troubled" (Ps. 88:1–2, NJB).

We are so much like the psalmist. Life for us moves between a hymn of praise and a lament of despair. Life is difficult to live, and far too often we collapse into one death or another in the midst of its demands. The windstorm deaths of teenagers, alienated lovers, despairing parents, and hopeless adults violently turn us around to face life again. We ask of ourselves and our communities the hard questions of fidelity and faithfulness. The writer Anthony Padovano declares:

> Life, life is what you must affirm, no matter how painfully, even unwillingly. . . .You are reliable only when others ascertain they will always find life in your presence. Others must know you as faithful, faithful so often that when they wonder where life lives, they will think of you as one of those in whom life has made a home.[3]

When we perceive suicide to be an act of hopelessness, we turn to the question of our own faithfulness and the sureness of life itself. In those searching times we pause to ask whether or not life finds a home in us and in the places and communities where we live. As we ask these questions and seek their answers, we find that God's redemptive work happens within and among us in ways more mysterious than we can comprehend or say. These windstorm deaths often become wings of transformation and flames of rebirth for those of us who remain.

Somewhere between the wind of deaths fully and clearly chosen and the fire of deaths tragically and desperately perceived, there are sandstorms that leave us with swirling challenges and beckoning glimmers of hope, political suicides that protest injustice and give witness to a new vision, self-giving deaths of middle-aged adults who firmly believe that life has run its course. These deaths, too, are oftentimes messengers and servants that we do not fully understand, and yet they are not easily dismissed. When we take every death seriously, it will always call all that we do and all that we are into question.

The psalmist stands beside us and proclaims anew God's eternal presence and asks us to embrace our Creator, one who comes to us as a spring gushing forth in the valleys, as a

---

[3] Miriam Therese Winter, *God-with-Us: Resources for Prayer and Praise* (Nashville: Abingdon Press, 1979), p. 83.

drink that quenches every thirst, as one who is clothed with majesty. But the psalmist's claim upon us is never that simple, for we are also charged to bless and celebrate the God who comes to us as wind and loves us as refining fire. When we plummet to the depths of what suicide really means, for a moment our simplistic answers are diminished, our religious piety is silenced, and our moral certainty is shaken. In these moments God moves in redemptive ways, calling us to throw our arms around the windstorm and let it cut grooves and holes and carvings into the very canyon walls of our souls.

*Laurence Hull Stookey* is Professor of Preaching and Corporate Worship at Wesley Theological Seminary. He holds degrees from Swarthmore College, Wesley Theological Seminary, and Princeton Theological Seminary. He is the author of numerous books and articles on preaching, worship, and hymnology.

This sermon grew out of rather unique circumstances. The author, although newly ordained at the time, was not new to the congregation, having served it in a student capacity for the five previous years. On the Thursday before the sermon was preached, he received word of the self-inflicted death of Dr. Doe, prominent pastor of a nearby church. Dr. Stookey had announced and prepared a sermon for this occasion, but decided at the last moment to deliver this sermon instead.

The sermon was preached in 1962. Dr. Doe had participated in the service at which the author was ordained the previous Sunday morning; on the evening of the ordination day, Dr. Stookey had been honored by a reception in his parish and at the time had made remarks about the nature of the ordained ministry, to which he alluded in this sermon.

# 10

# Toward
# a Christian Understanding
# of Suicide

## Laurence Hull Stookey

There are times when a pastor has prepared a sermon and suddenly finds it must be set aside to speak to another matter at hand. Such is the case this morning. This close to the observance of Aldersgate Day, I had intended to read a series of passages from the journal of John Wesley and to consider their meaning to us in light of his religious experience and ours.

John Wesley can wait. I feel constrained this morning to talk with you concerning the death of one of the leading Methodist pastors in our area. I do this regretfully—but with good reason, I think.

Some of you did not know Dr. Doe. He was the pastor of the Methodist Church in Churchville for the past eleven years. He was a leader in our Conference and was greatly respected by his fellow clergy. He was only forty-one years of age, yet he had served in key positions of leadership in our area.

For several years Dr. Doe chaired the committee that oversees the training and screening of candidates for the ordained ministry. Those of us who went through the process of preparing for ordination were fond of him and respected his leadership and character. He was so highly respected that last year he was one of three persons from this area elected as delegates to the national legislative assembly of our denomination, the General Conference.

Those of us who knew Dr. Doe saw him last week at the Annual Conference session. He seemed in good health and excellent spirits. I carried on several conversations with him at that time.

Naturally we were shocked to learn on Thursday of this week that Dr. Doe was dead. You will undoubtedly read of his death in the county paper, if you have not already learned of it from another source. I take the time this morning to mention the matter, for you may find yourself bewildered and perplexed by his death. For on Thursday morning of this week, Dr. Doe hanged himself in the basement of the parsonage.

This raises a problem which I suppose is as old as the church itself: How shall Christians react in the face of suicide? And the problem is writ particularly large before us when the deceased person was a respected minister of the Gospel. What, then, do we say?

In the face of suicide, more so than at any other time, the church is called upon to be compassionate and understanding. The great temptation is to throw up our hands in horror and cry out, "Suicide!" But our horror needs to be tempered with understanding.

Fortunately, contemporary psychology has helped us greatly at this point. Fifty years ago, suicide was considered to be the unforgivable sin by the Christian church. Many clergy refused even to conduct funeral services for those who took their own lives. Medical study takes a different attitude—one of understanding suicide as the result of mental distress, which merits sympathy, not condemnation.

It was once supposed that all suicide was the result of the spiritual degeneration of the soul—that it was virtually a punishment from God sent upon hopeless sinners. Now, in some cases the taking of one's own life *may* be the consequences of severe spiritual illness. I do not doubt that some persons, having wandered far away from

God, see no reason to live. But that is not the only possibility.

Many more cases of suicide, I believe, spring from a mental imbalance—sudden or gradual—than from the state of one's relationship with God. I have heard one or two psychiatrists say that no one who is really a Christian should ever end up in a mental hospital, much less as a suicide statistic. But that is by far a minority opinion—and one I personally cannot accept. Factors that are environmental, biological, and chemical in nature often influence us in ways we cannot explain or even detect.

In light of this, the Christian is in no position to judge the true cause or the motivation of suicide. It may be the result of some hidden sin that the person cannot face. Or it may be a sudden impulse which seemingly comes out of nowhere and cannot be resisted. Certainly suicide is not a natural instinct. Our basic instinct is to preserve our own lives at all costs. Suicide often, then, seems to be the result of an overpowering emotional or physiological disturbance.

I cannot think otherwise in the case of Dr. Doe. He left no suicide note, and there seem to have been no hints that would have caused anyone to predict, or enabled anyone to prevent, such an end. It is not for us to say, "There must have been some hidden reason, some great scandal in his life which no one knows." When the church faces such an instance of suicide, it behooves us to leave all judgment in the hands of the One who alone can judge the heart and mind. And as this One is the God revealed to us in Jesus Christ, we can expect divine mercy to be at work in abundance.

So much for our attitude toward Dr. Doe himself. But what about our attitude toward his family? Here again, we are called upon to be helpful and understanding. Oh, how the church fails at this point! Such tragedies make us uneasy and uncomfortable, so we think of all sorts of reasons for doing nothing.

Even we who are clergy are afflicted with a lack of compassion. I have heard preachers who have a heyday at the funerals of suicide victims. I have heard them preach hellfire-and-damnation sermons and warn that all of the mourners will end up in the same condition unless they speedily repent.

But where is the spirit of Jesus, who did not condemn even the adulterous woman, but rather forgave her in sorrow? It wasn't the sinners Jesus condemned. It was the hard-hearted, insensitive religious leaders who had no mercy upon the helpless and the distressed.

To extend the hand of human compassion, tenderness, and helpfulness: Is not this the mission God gives us?

But there is yet one more facet of this matter. The fact that the death of a pastor by suicide shocks us even more than someone else's suicide only sets in bold relief what I said to you last Sunday evening—namely, that ordination does not make clergy a different breed of people. Clergy have the same frailties and temptations common to all. In fact, I am inclined to say we have more frailties and temptations, for we are always dealing with the spiritual problems of others and, in the process, may become negligent about ourselves.

A pastor bears the burdens of the entire flock. The sorrows, the griefs, the distress of the whole congregation can become to the careful pastor a special burden. So I want to underscore what I also said to you last Sunday evening: that the pastor cannot do an effective work without full congregational support and encouragement.

How many congregations cause their pastors undue strain and grief! I am not speaking now from personal experience, for you have always supported me in every way. But I know student pastors who return to seminary each week literally in tears because of the fights, pettiness, and bitterness encountered over the weekend in their congregations. If congregations could know how a pastor's heart is torn in shreds by a congregational fight, I think many senseless feuds would be avoided. The congregation is charged with supporting the pastor, praying for the pastor, and helping to bear the burden of the one who leads them.

In the Roman Catholic service, at one point the priest turns to the congregation and says, "Brethren, pray for me." Perhaps in Protestantism we ought to do the same, knowing that we cannot endure without those prayers.

I am not in the least way suggesting that the Churchville congregation was torn apart by fights, or that the people there neglected to pray for their pastor. I am certain that neither is the case. I am simply suggesting that neglect along such lines can be one cause of tragedy among the clergy.

Several years ago, an article in *Life* magazine started quite a controversy. It was entitled "Why Ministers Crack Up." Many readers were shocked to learn that we do! Never forget, brothers and sisters, that we too are human, and in some ways more prone to human trials and failures than others may be.

Regardless of who your pastor is, now or in the future, do not withhold your support, but seek to help in every possible way. In at least some cases, tragedy may be avoided when congregations are sensitive to the needs and strains put upon their pastors. Let me say again that this is not a personal plea on my behalf, for I have no complaint against you. I simply note this as a word to be remembered in the future.

The church is called in all things to be a place of understanding and compassion. The church is to be a place where any and all can come with their difficulties and their problems, their fears and their failures. In the situation before us now, as in all situations, we are to leave judgment to God and be ministers of love and understanding to the weak and the distressed. To that end, let us pray to the Lord.

*Paul E. Van Dine* is Senior Minister of Cypress Lake United Methodist Church in Fort Myers, Florida. Born in Bluffton, Indiana, he grew up in Florida and graduated from the University of Miami and the School of Theology at Drew University. His prayers and sermons have appeared in several journals.

Some of the circumstances which precipitated this sermon are incorporated in the sermon's opening paragraphs. The pastor had known of six parish families who had endured the agonies of suicide by one of their members.

# 11

# When Pain Is Too Much

*Judges 16:25–30a; John 15:12–17*

## Paul E. Van Dine

There is a subject for which the time has come! It is time to rethink something of Christian history and test certain strands of Christian conviction. It is time to deal with a topic for which the textbook has not yet been written. It is time to turn over in our thoughts some issues for which final conclusions have not yet been reached. It is time to reconsider old attitudes that may be hiding somewhere in our hearts, disturbing and disrupting and destroying our better thinking on some very emotional issues of life and death.

It is time to talk of suicide and mercy death and God. What is the interplay among these three significant terms from daily affairs—suicide, mercy death, and God?

If your life has not yet been touched through self or child or grandchild, or niece or nephew, or spouse, or parent, or close friend having confronted one of these extremes in heart or fact, you probably have turned your eyes away. Seldom is life lived today untouched by these concerns!

Eight of every one hundred youths in school, twelve to eighteen years of age, attempted suicide last year, according to a study in Michigan reported in our local paper just last week.[1] Meanwhile, at the more mature end of life, Dr. Robert Butler, described as one of America's foremost experts on gerontology and winner of a Pulitzer Prize for his book entitled *Why Survive? Growing Old in America,* reminds us that "Up to 25 percent of all suicides are committed by persons over 65. The highest rate," he says, "occurs among white men in their 80's."[2] And these reports do not reflect at all the growing awareness about people seeking the release of death for themselves or their loved ones in times of terminal weakness, deterioration, disease, or pain.

Yes, it is a subject for which the time has come, this interplay between questions of suicide, of mercy death, and God! There is so much confusion, so much struggle to find peace and answers. The church—you and I—we are all derelict in our duty if not considering, if not sharing and discussing more freely and openly this circumstance and our God. But it has been as though we have hidden away for so long from the whole of it.

Let us here resolve together to be so and to do so no more! Let us share, let us minister to one another more openly and caringly on these subjects as on all others, where the deep things of life and hurt and God intersect.

Every sermon, of course, has a beginning. And on this occasion, I thought it worthwhile to share with you not only the message but the nature of its forming and its birth. Few sermons on crucial subjects (at least in my case) simply start and pop out at instant notice. Rather, something may lurk in the back of the mind for years, needing to be shaped and addressed before more current situation gives the subject birth.

My commitment to this topic probably began a couple of years ago when, on two separate occasions about a week

[1] Fort Myers (Florida) *News-Press,* May 14, 1986.

[2] Quoted in *The Christian Century,* May 8, 1985, p. 467; *U.S. News & World Report,* July 2, 1982, p. 51.

apart, I was counseling on the phone an unknown tearful voice, seeking reassurance about the soul of someone she loved. Suicide, for that one, had come.

I would not share publicly even this unidentifiable word about her grief if, in the first place, I had the least idea who she is or if, in the second place, I did not know her worries and fears and her grief are, unfortunately, so common

To my knowledge, I never met her face-to-face. She is only a voice on the anonymous telephone, whom I could not describe at all. But I had to reassure her again and again that my God is a God of grace and love beyond all else, and that while we may not understand the tragic act that leads someone to his or her death and so often causes such hurt to others, God understands the hurt we do not see. God surrounds with love that unmeasured and immeasurable pain of mind and body and soul that convinces someone they can endure no more.

Yes, God knows our hurt. God cares for it in its very worst extremities. I hope she understood this, wherever she is. And to anyone else who needs to hear this word, I hope you understand my God. The need to say this publicly perhaps first took form, therefore, in those phone calls a few years back.

A more immediate nurturing of this sermon's birth has been the publicity these past few weeks, bringing to consciousness both in the secular and in the religious press these issues of life and death—and the fact that, too much, such questions remain not only unsettled but unconsidered, never discussed openly in church. I had concluded, therefore, to speak several days before the *News-Press* conveniently brought the subject home this week with relevant reports on two different situations.

A third spur came on a much more positive side. Karen Appleby, one of our officers and members here, recently gave me a wonderful novel entitled *Cold Sassy Tree,* by Olive Ann Burns. It is a story about small-town life in

Georgia in 1906. With certain adjustments related to southern culture, however, it could be small-town life in that year just about anywhere.

This book deserves your reading. As I told Karen before I read it, it is in seminary bookstores and on many seminary reading lists. It is precious to me, however, because she said it reminded her of me and my sermons. And now that I have read it, I am so proud of her observation, I don't quite know what to do, for she was right. Here in this book is my God—the one I have preached in sermons she has heard—and I am glad the message gets across.

Old Grandpa Blakeslee is a businessman in that Georgia town—Cold Sassy is its name. But he preaches a mighty good sermon, by my thought and agreement, at the very least.

At one point in the story, his son-in-law commits suicide. Now, Grandpa Blakeslee and this son-in-law have not been exactly close. But against all the community sneers and hypocrisy over suicide, Grandpa insists upon a Christian burial.

Afterward his grandson, talking in the evening at Aunt Loma's home, asks "if he thought that Uncle Camp could of got to Hell already." His grandpa told him to shut up such thoughts and listen.

> "They's plenty men thet are mean and hateful son," grandpa said, "or they cheat folks, or beat their wives and their colored, but when they die, them preachers cain't say enough nice thangs. Well, Camp, he warn't evil or hateful, either one. He jest couldn't do nothin'. So doggit, Will Tweedy, ain't you or nobody else go'n say he's gone to Hell. He jest couldn't stand it no more. Would a lovin' God kick a boy unhappy enough to do what pore Camp did?"[3]

Yes, Grandpa Blakeslee's God is my God. I'm proud that people like Karen saw it without my saying so. But that, too,

---

[3] Olive Ann Burns, *Cold Sassy Tree,* p. 334.

was a reminder to me that some messages like this need to be said, and they need to be said from the Christian pulpit behind the full authority of this sacred desk, not merely seen by insightful persons indirectly in other things I say. That's my God. And that's how this sermon was born.

But now where, why, how can we say such things? To say that, as Grandpa said it in the book, requires us to go against at least one stream of Christian tradition and against some voices (and great voices, like Dietrich Bonhoeffer) in contemporary Christian ethics and debate. Bonhoeffer declared, "Even if a person's earthly life has become a torment for him, he must commit it intact to God's hand, from which it came."[4]

Thomas Aquinas argued, "Suicide is the most fatal of sins because it cannot be repented of" (*Summa Theologica* 2-2, question 65). And Dante placed suicides in the seventh level of hell, below that reserved for the greedy and the murderous! (*Inferno* 13).[5]

John Wesley, the founder of Methodism, is equally horrifying on this issue, calling suicide a "horrid crime" and urging its prevention by a law to the effect that those guilty should have their dead bodies publicly "hanged in chains."[6]

Thank the good Lord, Wesley himself realized human blindness, and he agreed that people could have differing Christian opinions from his own. Still, all of these opinions show us the source of the general attitudes around us in society, which many people conceive to be "the only" Christian view.

To Wesley's credit, the major thrust of his writing and intent was not the condemning of suicide itself, but the prevention of such tragic loss of life.

---

[4] Dietrich Bonhoeffer, *Ethics,* pp. 124–125.

[5] Quoted by William E. Phipps, "Christian Perspectives on Suicide," *The Christian Century,* Oct. 30, 1985, p. 971.

[6] John Wesley, *Works,* 3rd ed., vol. 13, p. 481.

And this, indeed, is a point to be kept in mind. The Christian spirit should not "bless" this idea of suicide with such grace that those otherwise never considering it, or at least never giving in to it, would be led by too easy a consideration of it into a tragic way out of merely problem circumstances. We—or I, at least—should not be presuming to suggest suicide is a normal and acceptable answer to jilting by girlfriends, or the shame of unwanted and unwed pregnancy, or financial reverses, or even the tragedy of much catastrophic illness. Usually, I am certain, if the person can be led to them, other solutions can restore something of meaningful, significant life!

We are *not* saying suicide is an ordinary, everyday decision or concern. It is not to be classed as one of many choices we make while going through life, like marriage or career.

It is a decision of a crisis of some kind—a decision of weighing values we have against one another, and of feeling hurts, or experiencing pain—pain that may or may not be noticeable to someone else. Everything possible should be done to notice people in their hurting extremities of life or shame, to hear their sorrows, to offer our own care, and to suggest new perspectives on it all. Usually, the perceived despair or sorrow or conviction of futility by the person can have a brighter prospect from another view, or with a little help. Life is not to be taken lightly, or given up easily. We are not saying so!

What I say, rather, is that none of us sees the hurt through the sufferer's eyes. None of us feels the embarrassment and shame of those who hold such heavy burdens on their souls. We cannot readily imagine the mental or physical burden that leads some people to this end.

But I am convinced that God does. My God is the one of whom it is written in other contexts, "he has borne our griefs and carried our sorrows" (Isa. 53:4). "My soul is bereft of peace, I have forgotten what happiness is," says the book of Lamentations. "But this I call to mind . . . : the steadfast love of the Lord never ceases, his mercies never come to an end" (Lam. 3:17, 21–22).

This is the God I always want to proclaim to you—the God who understands, who knows our deepest hurts and most stubborn sins, but who still cares, still loves, still reaches down and redeems us in the deep and hard places of our life. This is my God. I hope also it is yours.

I would be the last to suggest that suicide is a reasonable way out of most situations, but I hope I would be among the first to understand. For I know God is!

Now, briefly, the other part of this strange twofold subject we consider together here this morning is mercy death, in the sense either of suicide oneself, when facing terminal, possibly painful, or very costly lingering illness; or what has also come to be called mercy killing, involving others, by the removal of extraordinary life support or even feeding tubes in hospital situations; or giving suicide assistance to loved ones who are facing such pain or lingering deterioration and death.

It is hard, in one sense, to bring such cases together in any generalized consideration, for each is individual and particular. In one such case of local interest involving a husband taking the life of a wife, the judge scorchingly denounced it as "murder" and proclaimed his duty to prevent it and see to the punishment of the same.

Perhaps it is! Perhaps it is. For certainly this too is not an issue to be decided lightly. Law must always be worded in the best way possible both to defend public concerns and to protect individual rights. No one has a right to take another life without that person's consent, obviously—except, presumably, the state, in the interest of the common good.

Yet, as most of us are aware, the focus of discussion of controversial court cases in the world today usually is upon situations of *consent*—consent by the individual to the ending of his or her own life, or the carrying out of those kinds of wishes for someone else, either passively, by medical teams removing treatment, or actively by collusion of friends, family, or sympathetic medical personnel.

We cannot even begin in the scope of this sermon to

mention the intricate and important differences between "active" and "passive" euthanasia, or mercy death. Passive death, allowing death to occur, gradually has been gaining much acceptance over the last twenty years or so, acceptance in law as well as approval in the public eye, while "active" mercy death remains either condemned suicide or murder in most legal situations. Yet as Friday's newspapers showed us, even here half our populace grants approval to outright suicide by the terminally ill, and one may presume a growing sympathy for what may be called "assisted death," even though it is still in most instances statutory murder.

Now, where can some guidelines of Christian ethics be drawn amid the differing attitudes and medical circumstances in our day? I must leave us with unanswered questions here, but I want to suggest some directions, which I hope and trust are Christian, toward the basis for pursuing some solutions.

The first point is a recognition of the imperfection of the human mind and judgment and technology, and the ever-present possibility that tomorrow may offer hope or cure for us, a hope for a future not known today. I obtained permission in this regard from one of our members to share with you her story of living this past year under the diagnosis of incurable and inoperable cancer, from which she was not expected to live six months. Yet within the last few weeks, her condition has become such that a reevaluation had to be made. And the conclusion reached is that she did not have terminal cancer to begin with. Rather, she has been suffering from the perils and pains of a gallbladder infection! She and I, therefore, are two people who would remind everyone: In the worst of circumstances, don't give up on hope and prayer.

The second factor is always to remember the corruptibility of the best of us. Christianity calls it the doctrine of original sin. But what it means is, none of us acts completely free of selfish interest or concern. Families may be selfish, looking for inheritance or merely relief from responsibility or expense. The medical profession may be selfish, looking for anything from personal enrichment through fees to a sense of pride and worth from keeping a patient alive for one more hour or week. Our motives can be thus so mixed with good and ill, unconsciously and with the best of professed intent, that any decision to terminate life must be critically examined for such selfishness instead of good.

Yet a third factor, frequently overlooked, especially on the Christian and legal side, is that in our heritage and in the Bible, *life is not the absolute.* Love is. Caring is.

In our Old Testament text for today, Samson brought death upon himself as he stood in disgrace before his tormentors. Most of you have read or seen on television that the Jewish defenders of Masada took their own lives rather than turn themselves over to Roman hands. And we are aware that Christ, too, surrendered himself to die upon the cross rather than avoiding death to preach another day. Did you know that Eusebius, an early Christian writer, when celebrating the martyrs at Antioch, praised a mother and her two daughters who drowned themselves deliberately rather than submit to a Roman soldier's rape? These women who took their own lives rather than face a painful, humiliating, distasteful situation were recorded in Christian history before the time of Augustine as great martyrs of the faith!

Now, none of these persons lived in our times, and we do not live in theirs. The circumstances are different. I raise these examples only as testimony to the truth that in Christian history life is not the only value, not the only choice. There are values, we declare, that can even come into conflict with human life. Some things in Christian history always have been worth the loss of life itself. The question becomes, therefore, not *Can* life be taken? but *When* can life be given up?

At a preaching seminar recently, the Rev. Peter Whittier, one of our Florida ministers, described a girl, some twelve years of age, who was entering that time of young friendships, inviting others over, yet with heightened sensitivity and embarrassment, needing things to be just right. She always had been embarrassed about her mother's arms. And now the situation became crucial. Can't anything be done? she thought. Can't they be made prettier?

"We've done what we can afford," her mother said. "They're strong and good. I don't mind."

"Well, what happened, anyway?" the daughter asked. "Why are they like this?"

The mother had never talked about her arms and was not anxious to do so now. "Oh, you don't need to know," she said.

"Tell me! I am twelve years old! I'm old enough. You don't have to keep secrets anymore. Who hurt you? How did you get this way? Tell me!"

"When you were an infant," the mother finally said, "and asleep one day in bed, a fire broke out in our home. When I came through the doors of the nursery, the curtains were in flames, and they fell, burning, into your crib. I had to get them out."

And all of a sudden, her mother's scarred and disfigured forearms, which had been an embarrassment to this twelve-year-old girl, became a mark of beauty and love. "There is no greater love than this," declared Jesus in our text today, "than to lay down one's life for those one loves."

Can it be that these principles of Jesus have relevance when a man would rather pass on an inheritance to a child than exhaust it in a hospital? Can it be that these words of Jesus have relevance when an aged couple would each rather die than see the other watch his or her suffering and live on in pain?

I cannot presume today to suggest to you that I have the answers to all such questions of life and death as are faced now, in our homes, in society, and in law. But I do dare to suggest that, WHEN those answers are struggled with and found, it may be that in some instances the laying down of life is more loving than keeping it.

"Greater love has no one than this, that a man lay down

his life for his friends." It will be the task of the church, the law, and, most of all, the inner values of our souls to be sure that such love is possible, and not condemned by insurance regulation, court, or pulpit!

For God is apparently on the side of those who would lay down life itself for others. We dare not be on the opposite side!

*Paul T. Wachterhauser* is a graduate of Michigan State University and Garrett-Evangelical Theological Seminary and holds a master's degree in counseling from Central Michigan University. He is Associate Pastor on the staff of First United Methodist Church in Ann Arbor, Michigan.

Rev. Wachterhauser became aware of concern about suicide as he talked with suicidal counselees themselves, and with those who were worried about others who were threatening to take their own lives, and as he conducted funerals for victims of suicide and ministered to their families and friends. This sermon was preached to bring the subject into the light of day and to minister to the church about this painful and emotional issue.

# 12

## When Hope
## Abides in Suicide

*Jeremiah 18:1–6; Matthew 27:3–10*

## Paul T. Wachterhauser

Some have suggested that I must be suicidal myself to preach on such a subject, especially on Memorial Sunday. People want to enjoy coming to church, and suicide is such an unpleasant, unattractive, ethically complicated if not emotion-laden topic that it must be professional suicide for a minister to want to wade into it. I don't think so, because the church wants and needs relevant preaching, because Jesus did not shrink from relevant preaching, and because we need help in dealing with suicide. We believe the Christian gospel can address this need just as much as it addresses all of the rest of life and human experience.

Suppose I were to ask you to stand if ever in your life you considered about suicide, or thought about it rather seriously. (I won't do that.) Suppose I asked you to stand if you ever attempted suicide, or attempted it more than once. I might call out for those whose lives have been affected by somebody else's suicide. Maybe you'd be challenged to confront the "family secret" or to think more directly about the crash that everyone euphemistically calls "the accident." I daresay most of us would be on our feet! This is a very real issue we cannot deny, and it is inside as well as outside the faith community. We still remember and talk about Jonestown. We ministers, in our studies, hear of suicide fairly often. Just within a stone's throw of our church are two buildings that we can no longer walk beside without heartfelt tinges of grief and shock, and on the evening news we may see prominent leaders on hospital-bound stretchers or politicians with revolvers at their heads. In short, I don't want to talk about suicide either, but I think that we had better!

Professor and pastor Howard Clinebell reported in the mid-1960s that if a hypothetical minister served a church of 500 adults which was a cross section of America at that time, 25 of the members would have been hospitalized for a major mental illness, 24 would be alcoholics, 50 would report being handicapped by some neurotic symptoms, and 115 would answer yes to the question, "Have you ever felt you were going to have a nervous breakdown?" Every other year, one member of that church would attempt suicide. That means that the average minister might conduct three of those difficult funerals in every charge of his or her career. Since Clinebell wrote, the figures have soared. The suicide rate for our young people—teens and college students—has just caught up with the rate for the population at large, 12 per 100,000 per year. For our elderly, it is more than twice that. The rate for young men is still climbing. By the time the sun sets tonight over America, seventy will be gone by their own hand. By the time we gather here again on Memorial Day, 32,000 will be gone, and just by the time I recite this hour's benediction, three.

As nearly as I can figure, the Bible mentions only seven suicides. Isn't it fascinating that the only suicide mentioned in the New Testament was that of one of the twelve disciples? We do not know whether Jesus had even been made aware of Judas's death. I think there is evidence that Jesus surmised that Judas would be suicidal. I do wish we had some record of Jesus' reaction to Judas's self-destruction—over the years it could have given better guidance to the church, which sometimes has dealt with suicide so judgmentally. He who wept over Lazarus surely would have wept all the more for his old friend, Judas! For us, it is enough to note that even Jesus had a suicide attached to his life experience, and before his own demise had to deal with its eventuality.

Judas's experience has some of the classic characteristics of suicide. For examples, the disciples would appear to have had no idea of what was going on in his head. This is like the suicide's typical ambivalence, two feelings at once ("I am okay, and I choose to live" and, on the other hand, "I am wretchedly miserable and hopeless and I wish to die"), which gives rise to family comments such as, "I cannot believe she has done this thing—just last night she seemed fine!" Ambivalence. To the eleven, Judas was probably fine with no raging inner turmoil. This also is characteristic. Christ knew.

> As they were at table eating, Jesus said, "Truly, I say to you—one of you will betray me, one who is eating with me." They began to be sorrowful, and to say to him one after another, "Is it I?" He said to them, "It is one of the twelve, one who is dipping bread into the dish with me. For the Son of Man goes as it is written of him, but woe to that man by whom the Son of Man is betrayed! It would have been better for that man if he had not been born."
>
> Mark 14:17–21

Piercingly, while the others were blind, Jesus saw into Judas's heart. In the words of a hymn by John Greenleaf Whittier, "Our thoughts lie open to thy sight, and naked to thy glance; our secret sins are in the light of thy pure countenance." And there is evidence that Jesus wants to thwart Judas's course! Let this be a partial answer to those who claim that Jesus himself was suicidal, for his standing defenselessly mute before Pilate, and so forth, not turning aside from his course toward Golgotha. Yes, we believe Jesus chose death, ultimately, but to call it mere suicide ignores the high nature of his altruistic mission. The appeal to Judas to turn around is there! It is in the warning, "Woe to that man by whom the Son of Man is betrayed!"

William Barclay calls this section in Mark "Love's Last Appeal." Jesus is saying, "Don't do it. You'll be sorry and you'll wish you'd never been born!" Barclay says that Jesus is "telling him in advance of the consequences of the thing that it is in his heart to do."[1] But Jesus knows he cannot finally stop Judas from any of his choices. This is our whole human condition. Our God gives us free will. God's love appeals to us, God's truth warns us; but there is no compulsion, no firm outside prevention, and we must take responsibility for our choices. Priest and counselor Eugene Kennedy puts it this way: "People who attempt suicide usually mean business and they usually stay at it until they are successful."[2] This applies to anything we really are committed to doing. Jesus had to love Judas, warn him, and let him go. Interestingly, Barclay goes on, in a radical leap, to suggest that Jesus was really preventing something closer to homicide that night in the upper room, instead of warning of anything like betrayal or suicide. For if the Eleven had known of Judas's plan to destroy the Christ, he might not have gotten out of the room alive!

Well, how do you go on living with the knowledge that you have been instrumental in the arrest, mistrial, conviction, and execution of the Son of God? How can one die with more real guilt than that? But simply because Judas was human, if his guilt hadn't led to self-destruction, many other factors could have. Suppose he lived in our own day. He might well have hanged himself if he matched this profile—a depressed male over forty, single, divorced, or widowed without close friends. If he lived alone, were alcoholic, had recently suffered a great loss, or were elderly and seriously ill, he would also fit the pattern. Not all depressives commit suicide, but all suicides have an element of depression in them. His might have been an accidental suicide. Many times, when a person is standing at the brink of death, still feeling ambivalent, if not leaning

---

[1] *The Gospel of Mark,* rev. ed. (Westminster Press, 1975), p. 335.
[2] *On Becoming a Counselor,* p. 239.

toward life, something goes awry and an accident takes place. Did you know that interviews with people who jumped off the Golden Gate Bridge and lived to tell about it reveal that most of them really did not want to die? Had he been a youth, Judas might have wanted attention, or may have been too immature to see beyond the present trouble, either to better days or to effective problem-solving. I'll say more about that soon.

Judas might also have wanted to punish somebody. Ironic, isn't it, how we may try to do that by hurting ourselves. It is akin to the feeling I remember as a child, when I would lie in my bed at night, after some kind of parental confrontation, thinking, Boy, I'll bet if I ran away from home [or died tonight] they'd really be sorry, they'd really miss me, then they'd appreciate me! Adults do it, too. They choose to die to sting us, and we are expected to live on in the agony of guilt, in the wake of their manipulative hostility.

Sociologist Jeanne Binstock argues that suicide rates go up in cultures in which it is made difficult for persons to express their aggression publicly or privately. In child rearing, for example, we often control aggression in children by squelching it, making the child shut up or go to his or her room, not to be seen or heard, thereby turning the aggression inward, where it magnifies and may become fatal.

Suicides punish. They also express altruism, like the soldier who saves his platoon by throwing himself on a grenade. They express political activism. We can all still envision the Buddhist monks in self-immolation during the Vietnam War. During another war, a twenty-three-year-old Japanese kamikaze pilot wrote to his parents, "Please congratulate me. I have been given a splendid opportunity to die. . . . I shall fall like a blossom from a radiant cherry tree. . . . How I appreciate the chance to die like a man!"

Judas could have been a farmer about to go bankrupt, wanting his family to have the insurance benefits in hard times. Suicide has many faces. Judas might have been a complete materialist, the kind of person who thirsts again and again for the things of the world that do not satisfy, rather than having living waters in the heart. The poet Edward Arlington Robinson has described this person:

> Whenever Richard Cory went down town,
> We people on the pavement looked at him:
> He was a gentleman from sole to crown,
> Clean favored, and imperially slim.
>
> And he was always quietly arrayed,
> And he was always human when he talked;
> But still he fluttered pulses when he said,
> "Good morning," and he glittered when he walked.
>
> And he was rich—yes, richer than a king—
> And admirably schooled in every grace:
> In fine, we thought that he was everything
> To make us wish that we were in his place.
>
> So on we worked, and waited for the light,
> And went without the meat, and cursed the bread;
> And Richard Cory, one calm summer night,
> Went home and put a bullet through his head.[3]

More drastically, Judas might have been a youth. Not long ago in Bergenfield, New Jersey, Cheryl, Lisa, and two friends, both named Tom, sat in their Camaro in a closed garage with the engine idling. Cheryl was still grieving the suspicious alcohol-related death of her friend Joe a few weeks before. The engine, of course, lived longer than did the four, who died within the hour and brought teenage suicide in this country to national attention overnight. Hot on the heels of that tragedy were numerous copycat suicides all over the country, in what psychologists call a cluster effect. Psychologist Herbert Hieburg writes, "After a suicide, there is always an increase in copycat deaths." Amazing! Whoever thought of suicide as contagious? With teens, it can be. The impulse to imitate is very powerful,

---

[3] Edward Arlington Robinson, "Richard Cory."

especially with the immature, who tend to romanticize adventure and recklessness.

Pamela Cantor is president of the National Committee for the Prevention of Youth Suicide, and she claims that much of the cause here is the unmet need for attention. Young people see someone who is basically a nonentity suddenly getting community acclaim, maybe even local or national television coverage, and, because of their immaturity, they do not think of life's actual end in death. They see only an end to a problem, an end to pain. Teen vision in especially myopic and narrow. Teens are not yet wise enough to know that hard times pass, and that many creative resources may be brought to bear to help them. They hear too clearly a clarion call from the Pied Piper.

Bill Schechner is chief correspondent for *Main Street,* an NBC television news magazine for teens. Of teen suicides he has written:

> Society has forced these young people to grow faster and face harsher pressures than previous generations; they have to deal with sex and drugs earlier; they must compete harder for places in college or jobs in a flat economy; they see that their chances for a good future are not as bright as those of their parents at the same age, and are often considerably dimmer.
>
> At the same time we have cut their support systems. Single-parent homes and homes where both parents work mean children often don't have close ties to parents who are busy and under pressure; families move more frequently, so neighborhood ties are weaker; institutions like school and church are either larger and less personal than they once were, or they're just not as important as they used to be. The result is that when teenagers face problems, they face them without adults they can comfortably turn to for support and guidance. So what seems like a senseless suicide actually has roots in the way we deal with teenagers, what we expect of them, and, in most cases, the facts of their lives. What teenagers do seems senseless to us only because of our ignorance of the realities of their lives.

Sidney Harris, writing in the *Detroit Free Press* a few years back, lends his voice to this issue:

> The plain fact of the matter is that many . . . parents do not regard or treat their children as persons, only as objects. They are concerned with what the child does, how he acts, what rules he follows, what marks he gets, but not with what he is. . . . By the time children reach adolescence, they no longer confide in their parents, because they know their parents are not interested in their inner life, only in the public attitudes and their conformity to the regulations.
>
> One of the paradoxes of modern parenthood is that mothers especially are too "nosey" and too involved at the same time. They pry into their children's personal affairs for the wrong reasons—not to get closer to the child's essence and achieve genuine intimacy, but to find out if "bad" or forbidden things are being done.
>
> The child soon realizes that this interest in his affairs has nothing to do with his genuine needs or fulfillments, but is only a form of police spying. . . . He becomes sly, deceitful, and expert in laying a false scent. A child is not an object to be manipulated, but an organism to be understood. Here, if anywhere, Buber's I-Thou relationship must obtain.

We in the faith community may be called upon at some time to intervene in somebody's terrible pain. We may need to bring the first steps of hope and healing, the first glimpse of a vision beyond the barrier where any hope but the release of death is totally invisible. We need to have many of our myths about suicide exploded. Consider the following:

1. People who threaten to take their lives very often do so. It is not true that if someone talks of suicide, he or she won't do it. In fact, human beings are always trying to tell the truth about who they are to the world. The faulty wiring is in our not hearing, or wanting to hear, real threats we are afraid of hearing!

2. If one attempt was unsuccessful, it does not mean the person was not really serious. Twelve percent of

persons who attempt suicide will try again within three months.

3. If most of the time the person seems just fine, you may be seeing only part of an ambivalence, only the good moods. Keep tuned for other vital messages as well; do not be afraid to talk about them.

4. Talking about suicide does not put ideas in somebody's head. Ideas are already there. Talking may well defuse a highly charged feeling and help the person gain mastery over it!

Other useful suggestions come from Eugene Kennedy:[4] *Don't overreact and panic;* it is up to you to think clearly so you can listen objectively and begin to offer alternatives and help. *Don't underreact;* we don't want anyone to think we don't take them seriously. *Don't do the wrong things,* like cajoling someone not to do it, talking down, or using insincere flattery. Trying to distract them by talking of other things is too dishonest; trying to get them interested in other things is vain. What is required is honest, courageous, caring talk! Steer them to professional help any way you can.

In all we do, we need a solid theological base from which to work. I think these tenets are secure: that life is a gift and it is fundamentally good. While in the stratosphere the weather is always fine, here beneath the clouds we experience ice and wind, fog and snow. Life is hard, and we need to help each other through. God's very real hope is often mitigated through us as God's ministers; and, finally, as William Sangster once put it, "When the shallow hopes of the world are all dead—hope on in God."

Unsuccessful suicides will say, as did this teenager, "I just want someone to understand what I'm feeling and try to relate to me. I don't really want to die; I just want to escape." That is a cry for us to give to each other what our God strives to give to us, what Carroll Wise called "the cry of the human soul—to be understood, and accepted." "O

---

[4] *On Becoming a Counselor,* p. 238.

LORD, thou hast searched me and known me! . . . Whither shall I go from thy spirit?" (Ps. 139:1,7).

When I was in seminary, I had a friend who used to argue vehemently that one's choice of suicide was just one's choice, and nobody had any right to intervene. If an ambulance raced up the street, he would chide, "Oh, I suppose there they go, hurrying some poor self-destructive victim to an emergency room where all the best of modern medical technology will come to bear, and they have no right to save that person . . . they have no right!" He had a point, though in retrospect I wonder about his mood of depression and the energy with which he defended that view so strongly! On one level, self-destruction is a private matter. But it is also illegal; and part of that illegality may well be society's recognition that one such death touches many others who live on with years of grief, and it does have a contagious dimension if given permission, and we want to protect ourselves from ourselves. Should we intervene? Clinebell says, "A minister is obliged to use persuasion, coercion . . . , even physical restraint if necessary to save a person bent on suicide. . . . The role of ministry is to interrupt the person's momentum, to encourage him to explore the probable consequences, and to consider alternatives."[5]

If suicides are indeed ambivalent, even at the brink of death, that they still lean toward life, that most do not want to die, that they want true understanding and answers and hope, then how can we sit back and just let death take its awful and final course? Jesus could hardly let deafness or blindness or leprosy or crippling or death itself pass him by without the healing and life-changing word. Can we picture Jesus standing behind Judas and saying, "Be my guest"? Our Lord is the Lord of *life,* the Son of the one God who made life and called it good. He came in human form to live, making life sacred, he came to touch life, making it

---

[5] Howard Clinebell, Jr., *Mental Health Through Christian Community* (Nashville: Abingdon Press, 1965), p. 130.

better, and to die that we might have freedom from sin and death, saying with the meaning beyond the words of the popular theme song from the television hit *M\*A\*S\*H* that we can take or leave suicide because it is ultimately painless anyway? I think it would be more like Jesus to say something like these words from the preacher Paul Scherer:

> I have a young friend who would never think of having you call her an atheist, yet she has a notion that when she gets tired of life she has a perfect right to end it. She believes in everything but life itself. And that's a sickening mess. She's got it on her hands, and she sees nothing wrong in chucking it. What of it if she doesn't care for it? Nothing—only that if Christ is true, [life] came one day from God, with all the long vistas of his own great life hidden in it. And I'll not be flinging mine back in his face . . . or flinging it around either, as I please; or just letting it rot—because I think there's no longer any point in it. . . . If life is as meaningless as we try to make it with our hearts, then there's not God in it! If there is [God in it], it doesn't matter ever so little how we *feel* about it; it is an unbelievably precious and incalculable and endless thing.[6]

Someone has observed that after most mistakes in life we can at least recoup something or rectify something, but suicide obliterates all possibilities. Judas again is a case in point. He had given the money back. He repented, Matthew says, of betraying a love he surely did not understand. For that love, even from the cross—especially from the cross— would not betray him, so all-sweeping is God's forgiveness, especially given repentance. This is a case in point for all of us—this is the same love and power we need for living, it is the same love we need to show each other. Sermons won't do this. In an hour of need, these words will be far away. But real, risking love can be the grounded hope that—in

---

[6] "God's Claim on Man's Mind," quoted in *Twenty Centuries of Great Preaching*, vol. 10, Clyde E. Fant, Jr., and William M. Pinson, Jr., Researchers (Waco, Texas: Word Books, 1971), p. 331.

our terms, anyway—can turn suicide to kingdomtide! And we can say with the shepherd of the Gospel parable, "Rejoice with me, for I have found my sheep which was lost!" (Luke 15:6).

*Wasena F. Wright, Jr.,* a native Virginian, is a graduate of Ferrum College, Randolph-Macon College, and Union Theological Seminary in Virginia. He received his Doctor of Ministry degree from St. Mary's Seminary and University, School of Theology, in Baltimore, Maryland. He is Senior Minister of the Centenary United Methodist Church in Portsmouth, Virginia. Dr. Wright is also a member of the American Society of Suicidology. He has led seminars and lectured on ministering to survivors of suicide and has organized a Suicide Survivors Support Group.

This sermon addresses one of the perennial questions asked by persons who have lost loved ones by suicide. It came out of the preacher's ministry, both to family survivors and to a larger number of parish ministers who made known their own uncertainties about the subject. At the same time, the sermon reflects his own personal struggle to discover what he believed about this very complex subject.

# 13

# Suicide:
# An Unpardonable Sin?

*1 Samuel 31:1–6; Judges 16:23–30;*
*1 John 1:5–7*

## Wasena F. Wright, Jr.

The phone rang in my office one morning. The caller was trying to locate my father. His sister's husband had shot himself and was at that moment in the operating room of the hospital where he had been rushed. His chances for survival were not good. Within the hour came the news of his death.

On another occasion, young people wandered through the church building on Sunday morning as though in a daze, after hearing the news as they arrived at church that a classmate and friend had taken his own life the night before.

Yet another time I received a phone call from a good friend, a member of my last parish, telling me that his wife was in the acute care unit of the hospital after taking an intentional overdose of pills.

The story is told over and over again, with changes only in the names and details. Suicide, the act of taking one's own life, happens every day. It is now the second leading cause of death among teenagers, second only to accidents. It is the third leading cause of death among young adults. Approximately eighteen to twenty children and young persons will take their lives every day this year in this country. And this says nothing about the many suicide attempts that will be unsuccessful or the deaths that will be attributed to accidents or overdoses of drugs that may actually have been suicides.

Wherever or however suicide occurs, it is tragic. It brings great sadness and confusion into the lives of all those involved in the life that is gone. The church ought to be there to symbolize the presence of Almighty God to those affected by the tragedy. The church ought to be there to assure loved ones that there is a loving God who cares and understands—One who was revealed in the person of Jesus Christ, who shared the grief of the family and friends of his friend Lazarus at the news of his death.

But from what I have observed on these tragic occasions, the church has often been more judgmental and more despairing than hopeful. I don't mean this as a condemnation of the church; the reason is probably that we are not sure what the church believes about suicide. We are aware of the usually unspoken, unofficial, "underground" doctrines of many churches—that one who completes suicide is lost forever. We have heard suicide called an unpardonable sin. But most church members are confused about the matter. And those of us who are supposed to be leaders in the church are not doing much to help our people understand the issue. So I have been studying and thinking, trying to reach some conclusions of my own about the subject. Let me share some of the results with you.

First, let's look at the scriptures.

There are references to, and accounts of, suicide in the Bible. Two of these were used in the scripture lesson this morning. The first is from 1 Samuel 31. This is the story of Saul leading his army to defeat in battle against the Philistines. Three of Saul's sons were killed in battle (evidently Ishbaal was not present). Saul himself was hard pressed, wounded, and in despair. He was not afraid of being killed by the Philistines, but of being captured and taken back as a prisoner to be an object of mockery and shame. Saul asked an aide to kill him, but he refused. So Saul took his own sword and fell on it, taking his own life. Then his aide saw what Saul had done, and he fell upon his sword and died also.

The second reading is from Judges 16, the last part of the story of Samson. Earlier comes the account of Samson and Delilah. You will recall how Delilah was able to learn that the secret of Samson's strength was in his hair. As he slept, Delilah had a man shave his head, and the Philistines were able to capture him. They blinded him and bound him, made sport of him and humiliated him. They gathered to make sacrifices to their god for delivering Samson to them, and at the height of their celebration they brought Samson out to humiliate him further. They tied him to two pillars that supported the temple and tried to make sport of him. You may remember how Samson prayed to God for strength that he might take revenge on the Philistines for taking his eyesight. With a surge of strength, Samson pushed on the pillars, shouting, "Let me die with the Philistines." The temple fell with devastating results, killing Samson and thousands of the enemies of Israel, assumed to be enemies of Israel's God.

I never thought of Samson's death as suicide until I read an article by Tina Richards in the March–April 1981 issue of *Your Church* magazine. Mrs. Richards, a church employee and free-lance writer, writes out of her own experience in dealing with her husband's suicide, and she shows some interesting insights.

She points out that Samson was not "ill." He knew exactly what he was doing and even asked God for the strength to do it—and God gave him the strength. He took his own life, yet in Hebrews 11:32–34 we are given names of some of the great men of the faith whose faith had enabled them to accomplish great things, and Samson's name is on that list.

There are several other cases of suicide recorded in the scriptures, including the suicide of Judas in the New Testament. Suicides happen at all times and at all places—including biblical times and places—and yet the subject is never directly addressed in the scriptures. There is no explicit condemnation of suicide in the Bible. Suicides occurred in the time of Jesus, but he never spoke out against them. And Christians have not always condemned suicide.

Second, let's take a look at the church's attitude toward suicide in history.

The early Christians' attitude toward suicide was one of acceptance, particularly when persecution made life unbearable for them. The apostles did not condemn the practice, which apparently was rather common. In fact, several motives for suicide were regarded very favorably. The suicides of the martyrs were not considered displeasing to God. Cyprian declared that the Christians were invincible because they did not fear death and did not defend themselves against attacks. Tertullian, addressing Christians in prison awaiting martyrdom, encouraged them to go to prison unafraid, citing some celebrated ancient suicides and reminding them that the joy that awaited them would enable them to endure the torture.

Religious fervor has led many persons to put an end to their lives so that they might sooner enjoy the bliss of paradise. Throughout history there have been accounts of mass suicides, including that which occurred at the fortress of Masada, where 960 Jewish occupants formed and executed a suicide pact as the Romans were storming the fortress. Another more recent example is the tragic mass suicide among the followers of the fanatic religious leader, Jim Jones, at Jonestown, where nearly a thousand men, women, and children drank poison.

If there is no explicit condemnation of suicide in the scriptures, how did we get the common church position that suicide is a sin—even an unforgivable or unpardonable sin?

Augustine was the first to denounce suicide. Unquestionably he shaped the later attitude of the church toward suicide as a sin. In *The City of God* he discusses the question at great length, pro and con. He concludes that suicide is never justifiable. He bases his opinion on the fact that suicide eliminates the possibility of repentance and is a form of homicide and therefore a violation of the Sixth Commandment. It is interesting that for the first 400 or 500 years of the Christian church, the Sixth Commandment, "Thou shalt not kill," was interpreted as meaning that one should not take the life of another.

Augustine found himself in a dilemma regarding some of the suicides that had already been canonized. The church had made saints of some who had committed suicide, so Augustine admitted certain exceptions. He said that some—St. Pelagia, for example—had received divine revelation which released them from rules applying to others.

In the fifth century, the church concurred with Augustine, and suicide was specifically condemned by ecclesiastical law. By the time of Thomas Aquinas, suicide was considered not only a sin but a crime as well. In his *Summa Theologica,* Aquinas formulated the attitude that the Roman Catholic Church holds to this very day regarding suicide.[1] The argument against suicide is deeply rooted in fundamental Christian doctrines, such as the sacredness of human life, the duty of absolute submission to God's will, and the extreme importance attached to the moment of death. Aquinas stressed the argument of Augustine that the person who deliberately takes away the life given by the Creator displays the utmost disregard for the will and authority of the Master, and, worst of all, does so in the very last moment of life when one's doom is sealed forever. This Aquinas regarded as "the most dangerous" thing of all because no time is left to expiate it by repentance. The

---

[1] *Editor's note:* Only in 1983 was canon law regarding final rites for suicides changed.

Roman Catholic Church never wavered from this pronouncement, and its power was so great that Christian Europe legalized its teachings. Those teachings, of course, were ingrained in the people who later came to America, and this is how the prevalent Christian feeling about self-destruction originated.

The eighteenth-century philosopher David Hume, in his famous "Essay on Suicide," examines all the arguments against suicide. He says, "If suicide is criminal, then it must be a transgression of our duty either to God, our neighbor, or ourselves." He concludes that a person who retires from life does no harm to society—but only ceases to do good, which, if it is an injury, is of the lowest kind. Hume insists correctly that not a single line of scripture prohibits suicide. Instead of interpreting the commandment "Thou shalt not kill" as a divine prohibition against suicide, he holds that it evidently meant to exclude only the killing of others, over whose life we have no authority.[2]

Also in the eighteenth century, the French author and philosopher Voltaire, though opposed on principle to the philosophy of despair, admitted that despair may be absolute and inescapable. In such cases, suicide may be defined as an act of necessity.

How then shall we view suicide?

My answer may not be the same as yours, but in light of my own study of the scriptures, theology, and religious tradition, I have reached some personal conclusions about suicide. It is important for a Christian to reach his or her own conclusions, for they will determine how one relates to the person who has attempted suicide and to the families of suicide victims.

Is suicide a sin? If I must give an answer, my answer is yes. I agree with Augustine that God is the Creator—the Giver of life. I believe human life is sacred because it does come from God. I believe we are given the gift of life for a

---

[2] David Hume, "An Essay on Suicide" (1777; reprinted Yellow Springs, Ohio: Kahoe & Co., 1929).

purpose—we are not here by accident. God has a purpose for each of us. We have our contribution to make to life. God knows, and we do not know, when the purpose is fulfilled and the contribution is ended. It is wrong for a person to take away a life God has given—whether it be one's own life or the life of another. So suicide is, for me, a sin.

But is suicide an unpardonable or unforgivable sin? Here I must answer with a resounding no! Suicide destroys the body, which ought to be a temple, but can scarcely blaspheme the Spirit.

Is swift suicide any worse sin than that of those of us who knowingly or ignorantly commit a slow suicide gradually by unhealthy living? Is not overindulgence—smoking, alcohol or drug abuse, or overeating—merely a form of self-destruction whereby we take years off our lives by the way we live? Can it be more sinful to take one's own life than it is to take the lives of others in war? Can suicide be more sinful than to allow millions to die of starvation while we have an overabundance of food?

If suicide is a sin, let us remember that we are all sinners in one way or another. None of us is perfect. None of us is without sin. But we have a God who offers us forgiveness, a God who loved us enough to come to us in person and lay down his life for the forgiveness of our sins. . . . Did you hear what I just said? Think about that: "He laid down his life" for us. In the tenth chapter of the Gospel of John, Jesus says,

> For this reason the Father loves me, because I lay down my life, that I may take it again. No one takes it from me, but I lay it down of my own accord. I have power to lay it down, and I have power to take it again; this charge I have received from my Father.
>
> John 10:17–18

If Jesus gave his life voluntarily that each of us might have life, could his death be suicide? If he laid down his life—if no one took it from him, could that be seen as suicide for the benefit of others? Then there must be the possibility of an act that is technically suicide but *not* a sin. Are there, as Augustine supposed, "exceptions"?

The real tragedy of suicide is not whether or not one repents. The real tragedy is that a person gets boxed in and feels such despair that he or she can find no way out. Paul Tillich, in the second volume of his *Systematic Theology,* writes,

> In despair, not in death, man has come to the end of his possibilities. . . . The pain of despair is the agony of being responsible for the loss of the meaning of one's existence and of being unable to recover it. One is shut up in one's self and in conflict with one's self. It is out of this situation that the question arises whether suicide may be a way of getting rid of one's self. . . . There is a suicidal tendency in life generallv, the longing for rest without conflict.[3]

Tillich says in another place, "Suicide actualizes an impulse latent in all life." In this he is in agreement with psychiatrists who say that almost everyone, at one time or another, has thought of suicide, though few actually commit it.

Arnold Bernstein, a psychoanalyst who frequently deals with suicidal people, wrote an article entitled "My Own Suicide." He says in this article that there are situations in life which could possibly make him commit suicide. He said something I believe is important for us to hear:

> I long ago surrendered that arrogance of believing that I am better than persons less fortunate than me. . . . We are all so much more fragile than we know, and our strength can dissolve into weakness with a turn of the wheel of fortune . . . because what we feel and do can hardly be understood apart from our past and present life circumstances. . . . We must all bear in mind, "There, but for the grace of God, go I."[4]

---

[3] Paul Tillich, *Systematic Theology* (Chicago: University of Chicago Press, 1967), vol. 2, p. 75.

[4] Arnold Bernstein, "My Own Suicide," in *Between Survival and Suicide,* ed. E. B. Wolman and H. H. Kraus (New York: Halstead Press, 1976), p. 56.

God knows our weaknesses. We are all so fragile, and we are hurt and inflict hurt so easily. We all need to be more loving and understanding in situations where this kind of tragedy has occurred.

Most Christians believe that the decision to end human life in this world is something that should be left up to God. Nevertheless, we must not become judgmental and arrogant at this point. Paul, in his letter to the Romans, calls us to live in the faith that nothing can separate us from the love of God in Christ Jesus. Listen to him:

> What then shall we say to this? If God is for us, who is against us? . . . Who shall separate us from the love of Christ? Shall tribulation, or distress, or persecution, or famine, or nakedness, or peril, or sword? . . . No, in all these things we are more than conquerors through him who loved us. For I am sure that neither death, nor life, nor angels, nor principalities, nor things present, nor things to come, nor powers, nor height, nor depth, nor anything else in all creation, will be able to separate us from the love of God in Christ Jesus our Lord.
>
> Romans 8:31, 35, 37–39

As I read over this list, I believe that death by suicide does not have the power to separate us from the love of God either.

The God I know and serve and worship loves and cares for everyone. God cares for the one who commits suicide and loves that person with a love that exceeds any form of earthly love. And I believe with all my heart that in judging that person God will take into account more than the manner of death.

Anyone contemplating suicide should read William James's essay entitled "Is Life Worth Living?" in which he deals with the question. James had been concerned with the subject since his youth. During his adolescence and early manhood he suffered from mental depression, which at times was so severe that it totally incapacitated him. In this essay, James makes his final appeal to religious faith. He says that life is worth living, no matter what it brings, provided one can continue the battle against oppression courageously. He says that frequently the only thing that makes life worth living is religious faith. He says, "If you surrender to the nightmare view of life and crown your unbelief by your own suicide, you have indeed made the picture totally black. Your mistrust of life has removed whatever worth your own enduring experience might have given to it." Then he issues his final challenge: "Be not afraid of life. Believe that life is worth living and your belief will help create the fact."[5]

Suicide is a reality. Many of us know of someone who has completed suicide. Most of us know someone who has attempted it. It is important that we consider the subject, because the way we view suicide will determine how we are able to relate to the family of the suicide victim or to one who has attempted suicide. We, as the people of God, need to be able to bring comfort and understanding to those who try to handle the emotionally shattering experience of suicide. It is not up to us to pass judgment. We leave that to a loving God.

Scripture, in 1 John 1:7, says: "The blood of Jesus his Son cleanses us from all sin." This assures us that no sin can place us outside the love of God as revealed in Christ Jesus our Lord, and I submit to you that suicide does not have that power either.

---

[5] William James, *The Will to Believe and Other Essays in Popular Philosophy* (New York: Longmans Green, 1904), p. 39.

# Conclusion

Here, then, are a baker's dozen of sermons on suicide, intended as a resource for preachers, religious educators, congregational leaders, and lay people. I hope that anyone having an interest in issues relating to suicide, whether because of personal experience, professional responsibilities, biblical and theological interests, or social and ethical concerns, will find these sermons a source of insight not available in other works. Books on suicide and the Bible, ethics, history, pastoral care, psychology, or sociology, however helpful they may be in their own way, do not give the broad and personal perspective that one finds in sermons.

## Biblical Texts

In these sermons, more than a dozen biblical passages are used as texts on which the sermons are based, with as many additional references mentioned in passing. Few people, even those who know the Bible well, would guess that this many texts could bear directly on suicide. They come from biblical literature that is historical (Judges, 1-2 Samuel, 1 Kings, Acts); liturgical (Psalms); and prophetic (Jeremiah). They include the words of Jesus (Mark and John) and the letters of Paul (Romans, 1 Corinthians, and Galatians).

Very few biblical texts relate to actual occurrences of suicide or attempted suicide—only seven actual accounts of self-chosen death, plus one or two suicide attempts. This small number underscores the fact that much of religious thought and decision-making is informed, not by specific biblical injunctions on a given subject, but by more general statements, stories, and prayers, which are interpreted in a way that relates them to a topic of current concern. This method is as old as the Bible itself and has been used by both Jewish and Christian interpreters throughout the centuries.

Approaching the Bible in this way does not do violence to it as a source of religious authority. What was said by the original authors for their own times must be applied in new ways to the new situations inevitably faced by later generations. This constant reinterpretation is absolutely necessary if any religious community is to keep the faith alive and well. Only when the original meanings are ignored entirely or the applications twisted beyond all reason do we have a form of interpretation that is inappropriate, unfaithful, and detrimental.

## History and Literature

Preachers are regularly drawn to use examples from both history and literature to explicate the ways in which biblical messages continue to apply to the lives of the faithful. In these sermons, references are made both to situations in history and to some of the world's great literature. Josephus, the fall of Masada, Eusebius, Augustine, Tertullian, Aquinas, Dante, John Donne, Hume, Voltaire, John Wesley, and William Cowper are among those that have been cited here.

One reason why preachers who address suicide turn to history and literature for illustrations is that most of the books and articles in dictionaries and encyclopedias themselves give attention to those areas. As the Introduction pointed out, one of the works most frequently consulted by students of suicide is Fedden's *Suicide: A Social and Historical Study*. It is filled with literary and historical references. Some contemporary art forms—plays, dramas, and video documentaries—are included in the suggested works for further reading.

To be sure, any rhetorical use of past accounts always runs the danger of weighting the evidence in favor of the point being made. Most any position can be supported from history, and certainly literature, if one makes a study of the subject in enough detail. Even so, the lessons recorded in the world's chronicles and the force of ideas detailed in poetry, drama, opera, letters, and essays, as well as the visual arts, continue to be very influential in shaping the thought of preachers and lay people. In this respect, the sermons here illustrate in a small way how twenty-five hundred years of literature have dealt with the subject.

### Statistics

In order to show the immediate relevance of a sermon on suicide, use has also been made of statistics. This is one of the most undervalued sermonic resources. Bill Holmes's opening remarks, like his sermon title, are graphic in their use of a basic set of reliable figures. They state—immediately, clearly, and forcefully—that the subject of the sermon is one of profound relevance for his entire congregation. Most of the other sermons also use statistics, which may vary, depending on when the sermon was preached.

Anyone reading in the field of suicide, or simply catching the news from radio, television, daily papers, or magazines, will quickly see how often the grim figures are cited. With a bit of imagination, even the most dry and seemingly irrelevant statistics can be brought home in striking ways. To take one frequently used example in another area, one can drop a single BB into a gallon bucket to represent all the firepower used in World War II from 1939 to 1945. One can then pour *six thousand* BB's into a large metal garbage can to illustrate the amount of nuclear firepower now available. To this incredible total, additional nuclear weapons are being added each year. Regrettably, this illustration is not totally unrelated to the subject of suicide. The prospects of a nuclear war have been observed in connection with the despair and hopelessness that many teenagers experience as they look to the future.

The statistics cited in these sermons are drawn from the areas of age, sex, class, vocation, race, method, and geography. All are basic to a thorough sociological study of the subject. The best resources for reliable statistics are the Centers for Disease Control in Atlanta and the U.S. Department of Health and Human Services. The list of Selected References provides several works where useful statistics may be found. Those wanting to make an even stronger sermonic point would also want to seek out data related to their own state, county, city, or parish.

Quite often, one of the most effective ways of putting the whole range of suicide issues in perspective is through the use of accurate figures. Indeed, apart from that empirical source, neither religious communities nor any other group can make a realistic evaluation of suicide and its consequences.

### Scientific Advances

Few factors have been so influential in effecting changes in attitudes toward suicide than the remarkable advances in the fields of sociology and psychology. The works of Émile Durkheim and Sigmund Freud launched serious research and study into the mysteries of society and of the individual people. The results of studies in these fields did much to remove the responsibility for suicide from the rational individual and prompted a less stringent attitude on the part of religious communities. Medical research about the effects of chemical imbalances and genetic influences has also prompted a rethinking along these lines.

At the same time, these advances have raised new ethical questions, many closely akin to those surrounding euthanasia. In all these matters, several of which are specifically mentioned in the sermons, preachers are reminded both of the need to be well-informed on current events and to see clearly the implications of advances in medical research.

## Ethical Issues

At the heart of any religious concern for suicide are the host of ethical issues that so easily arise. How one's own life is to be used, even in the choice of death, relates directly to one's relationship to the Divine, as well as to all one's significant others—family, friends, religious community, social cause, or state.

The complexity of the issues, and the obvious reluctance of many of today's churches (less so for most Jewish groups) to wrestle openly with that complexity is, I suspect, one of the major reasons why so few sermons are preached on suicide. The severely negative view that has dominated religious teaching since Augustine has not been reevaluated in the light of current psychological, sociological, and physiological research, except by a very few religious thinkers. As both Holmes and Wachterhauser have noted, a number of myths still prevail, including the one which holds that even to talk about suicide at all is to encourage it. Suicidologists are convinced of just the opposite. They insist that more, not less, information and open discussion are needed for the prevention of suicide. Only by addressing the issue and doing one's intellectual homework can any pastoral leader hope to meet the responsibilities related to suicide in an effective manner.

In the broad mix, ethical questions involve personal rights and intervention, state legislation, federal and military use of lethal pills, insurance practices, the proper use of time, energies, and money, and social stigma. A variety of ethical problems are specifically mentioned in these sermons.

Few congregations today can remain oblivious to at least some of the personal and social implications of suicide. Both media coverage and the reality of suicide in ever-widening circles of church and society bring several important questions to the forefront of our thinking. As these sermons well illustrate, the pulpit can be an effective vehicle for encouraging a long-neglected wrestling with the ethical questions that an increasing number of people in the pews are already harboring.

## Theological Issues

Ethical issues, however complex in themselves, are never discussed in a vacuum, at least not in religious communities. Always they are related to larger theological issues. What is the will of God? How is that will perceived? Is it inflexible, or are there changes in situations that allow or even dictate different responses? Can a loving, caring God overlook a life of goodness and faith because of one act? Does God understand better than we the real reasons why individuals act as they do?

There are also questions related to anthropology. Do human beings have permission, even the "divine right," to end life as they wish? Do they, in peculiar circumstances, have a *responsibility* to end it? Might one receive forgiveness beyond the ultimate act of suicide, or does that act in itself preclude human forgiveness? What is the chief end (teleology) of human beings, and how best might that end be accomplished?

Theological and anthropological questions surface often in these sermons. They call for intense reflection involving scripture, tradition, experience, and statistics, as well as medical and sociological insights. All must be used with carefully ordered reason. Funeral services are necessary and challenging and make important theological as well as pastoral statements. Nevertheless, they cannot provide the proper setting for all the needed explorations of faith. The context of a full worship service does, on the other hand, offer an occasion in every way suitable for religious communities to begin engaging in their theological task, and so to mature in its spiritual life.

## Personal Illustrations

Every preacher is taught from the beginning of Homiletics 101 that confidentiality is a sacred trust. What she or he learns about parishioners must not be repeated from the pulpit, even when that confidentiality was established years before in distant parishes. This well-known rubric of preaching certainly applies in sermons on suicide.

There are, however, ways in which the essence of personal stories can be told—as often as possible with the permission of those directly involved—without betraying the sacred trust. Several examples of the proper use of personal illustrations have been included here. They are models of how this basic sermonic resource can be used even when preaching on entirely different subjects.

## Pastoral Care

No aspect of suicide is more demanding than that of pastoral care. For every completed or attempted act of self-destruction, the pastor's work is multiplied by the number of friends and family directly involved. Added to this are all the dimensions of care to be given to the congregation, and often to the community. Madeline Jervis's sermon is a case in point.

For all the church's reluctance to meet the broader issues related to suicide, its best work has been done by pastoral counselors and medical personnel, those whose work has repeatedly brought them into direct confrontation with many aspects of the subject. The abiding tragedy is that religious leaders have not provided counselors and other professionals with the theological and practical support they deserve in dealing with this matter.

Pastoral care is a major theme sounded in several of the sermons here presented. Some speak to those contemplating suicide, while others focus on ways of helping survivors, both to understand the religious and psychological dimensions of suicide and to cope with their practical problems.

Today, as throughout its long history, the sermon can be a significant means of effecting genuine pastoral care. Preaching on suicide can accomplish several desirable goals in the essential tasks of ministry.

## Social Action and Community Response

One further dimension of the pastoral office reflected in these sermons is that of initiating social action and a response within the religious community. The role of church and synagogue in helping to change negative attitudes that affect society has a long history and remains a particularly challenging one in the current national crisis on suicide.

It can hardly be disputed that the church, particularly in Western civilization, has created many of the attitudes that have shaped our customs and prompted our legislation regarding suicide. Whatever horrors, abuses, and injustices Western society has heaped upon suicides, attempted suicides, and their families, and whatever social indignities and emotional scars have resulted, much if not all of the blame can rightfully be laid at the doorstep of the church.

We no longer approve of the disgusting practice of dragging the bodies of suicides through the streets and exposing them naked at the crossroads. But other forms of stigma persist and a number of punitive laws remain on the books. Many religious communities have yet to organize support groups. Ministerial associations have largely failed to discuss ways in which they might be more directly involved in the community to prevent suicide and to counsel those who survive. Actions such as these still need to be initiated by religious groups. Through well-informed, solid theological preaching, religious communities can be led to engage directly in both the theological reflection and the community action necessary for a vital faith.

## Summary

Over the past quarter century, America's pulpits have addressed dozens of crucial, challenging, and controversial subjects, among them nuclear disarmament, racism, sexism, abortion, ageism, euthanasia, ecology, the Vietnam War, and homosexuality. Preaching on these subjects has both prompted and resulted from a variety of responses by religious communities.

It is now time for those communities to give serious attention to the many dimensions of suicide and for pastors, priests, and rabbis to address the topic in their sermons. They must not be expected, nor must they expect themselves, to give the *last* word, but they can at least give what may be the *first* word, publicly, for a congregation. Ideally, that word will lead to Bible study, data gathering, informed debate, prayerful reflection, and courses of action in treatment of others individually and in social contexts. The sermon can be a significant first step in "building up the church" in the midst of a crisis that has been too long neglected.

It is a source of genuine satisfaction to review these thirteen sermons. Not only do they demonstrate that suicide *can* be used as a sermon topic, they also show that it *should* be! In the process, they provide a number of homiletical helps that will aid the preacher in meeting other ministerial tasks.

A close look at the kinds of physical, psychological, and social settings in which the sermons were preached provides a striking commentary on the kinds of challenges preachers face in the midst of the current crisis. This point alone is a clear reminder that religious professionals are among the significant gatekeepers of American society, as well as of their own communities of faith.

It is with the fervent hope and prayer that a much larger number of preachers will respond to the need for more sermons on suicide that I offer this work, confident that only in this way will church and synagogue be at their best in meeting the challenges of the current crisis.

# Selected References

## Books and Articles

Alvarez, A. *The Savage God: A Study of Suicide.* New York: Random House, 1972.

Baechler, Jean. *Suicides.* Tr. by Barry Cooper. New York: Basic Books, 1979.

Bailey, Lloyd R., Sr. *Biblical Perspectives on Death.* Overtures to Biblical Theology. Philadelphia: Fortress Press, 1979.

Battin, Margaret Pabst. *Ethical Issues in Suicide.* Englewood Cliffs, N.J.: Prentice-Hall, 1982.

_____, and David J. Mayo, eds. *Suicide: The Philosophical Issues.* New York: St. Martin's Press, 1980.

Bennett, John. "The Van Dusens' Suicide Pact," *Christianity and Crisis* 35, no. 5 (March 31, 1975), 66–67.

Berent, Irving. *The Algebra of Suicide.* New York: Human Sciences Press, 1981.

Bonhoeffer, Dietrich. *Ethics.* Ed. by Eberhard Bethge. Tr. by Neville Horton Smith. New York: Macmillan Co., 1965.

Burns, Olive Ann. *Cold Sassy Tree.* New York: Ticknor & Fields, 1984.

Cain, Albert C., ed. *Survivors of Suicide.* Springfield, Ill.: Charles C Thomas, 1972.

Clemons, James T. "Suicide," in Geoffrey W. Bromiley, ed., *International Standard Bible Encyclopedia,* Rev. ed., vol. 4, 652–653. Grand Rapids: Wm. B. Eerdmans Publishing Co., 1988.

_____. "Suicide and Christian Moral Judgment," *The Christian Century,* May 8, 1985, 466–469.

Coleman, Loren. *Suicide Clusters.* Winchester, Mass.: Faber & Faber, 1987.

Danto, Bruce L., and Austin H. Kutscher, eds. *Suicide and Bereavement.* New York: Arno Press, 1977.

Davis, Patricia A. *Suicidal Adolescents.* Springfield, Ill.: Charles C Thomas, 1983.

Donne, John. *Suicide.* (*Biathanatos,* transcribed and edited for modern readers by William A. Clebsch.) Chico, Calif.: Scholars Press, 1983.

Dunne, Edward J., John L. McIntosh, and Karen Dunne-Maxim. *Suicide and Its Aftermath: Understanding and Counseling the Survivors.* New York: W. W. Norton & Co., 1987.

Durkheim, Émile. *Suicide: A Study in Sociology.* Tr. by John A. Spalding and George Simpson. New York: Free Press, 1951.

Ellis, Edward Robb, and George N. Allen. *Traitor Within: Our Suicide Problem.* Garden City, N.Y.: Doubleday & Co., 1961.

Farber, Maurice L. *Theory of Suicide.* New York: Arno Press, 1977.

Farberow, Norman L. *Bibliography on Suicide and Suicide Prevention, 1897–1957, 1958–1970.* Rockville, Md.: National Institute of Mental Health, 1972.

————, ed. *The Many Faces of Suicide: Indirect Self-Destructive Behavior.* New York: McGraw-Hill Book Co., 1980.

Farberow, Norman L., and Edwin S. Shneidman, eds. *The Cry for Help.* New York: McGraw-Hill Book Co., 1961, 1965.

Fedden, Henry Romilly. *Suicide: A Social and Historical Study.* London: Peter Davies, 1938.

Gernsbacher, Larry Morton. *The Suicide Syndrome: Origins, Manifestations, and Alleviation of Human Self-Destructiveness.* New York: Human Sciences Press, 1985.

Giovacchini, Peter. *The Urge to Die: Why Young People Commit Suicide.* New York: Penguin Books, 1983.

Gore, Tipper. *Raising PG Kids in an X-rated Society.* Nashville: Abingdon Press, 1987.

Grollman, Earl A. *Suicide: Prevention, Intervention, Postvention.* 2nd ed. Boston: Beacon Press, 1988.

Gustafson, James M. *Ethics from a Theocentric Perspective,* vol. 2, *Ethics and Theology.* Chicago: University of Chicago Press, 1984. Ch. 6, "Suicide," 187–216.

Harran, Marilyn J. "Suicide," in Mircea Eliade, ed., *The Encyclopedia of Religion,* vol. 14, 125–131. New York: Macmillan Publishing Co., 1986.

Hendin, Herbert. *Black Suicide.* New York: Basic Books, 1969.

_____. *Suicide in America.* New York: W. W. Norton & Co., 1982.

Hewett, John H. *After Suicide.* Philadelphia: Westminster Press, 1980.

Hillman, James. *Suicide and the Soul.* New York: Harper & Row, 1964.

Hiltner, Seward. "The Pastor and Suicide Prevention," *Pastoral Psychology* 16, no. 160 (January 1966), 28–29. The subject is discussed in several articles in this number, for which Hiltner was the editor.

Housley, Kathleen. "Churches Respond to Teen Suicide," *The Christian Century,* April 30, 1986, 438–439.

Joan, Polly. *Preventing Teenage Suicide: The LIVING Alternative Handbook.* New York: Human Sciences Press, 1986.

Johnston, Jerry. *Why Suicide?* Nashville: Oliver-Nelson, 1987.

Kennedy, Eugene. *On Becoming a Counselor: A Basic Guide for Non-Professional Counselors.* New York: Seabury Press, 1977.

Kinast, Robert L. *When a Person Dies: Pastoral Theology in Death Experiences.* New York: Crossroad Publishing Co., 1984.

Klagsbrun, Francine. *Too Young to Die.* Boston: Houghton Mifflin Co., 1976.

Kreitman, Norman, ed. *Parasuicide.* London: John Wiley & Sons, 1977.

Kübler-Ross, Elisabeth. *To Live Until We Say Good-bye.* Englewood Cliffs, N.J.: Prentice-Hall, 1978.

Landsberg, Paul-Louis. "The Moral Problem of Suicide," in *The Experience of Death/The Moral Problem of Suicide,* 65–97. Tr. by Cynthia Rowland. New York: Arno Press, 1977.

Leonard, Calista V. *Understanding and Preventing Suicide.* Springfield, Ill.: Charles C Thomas, 1967.

Lester, David. *Why People Kill Themselves: A 1980s Summary of Research Findings on Suicidal Behavior.* 2nd ed. Springfield, Ill.: Charles C Thomas, 1983.

Linzer, Norman, ed. *Suicide: The Will to Live vs. the Will to Die.* New York: Human Sciences Press, 1984.

McManners, John. *Death and the Enlightenment: Changing Attitudes to Death in Eighteenth-Century France.* Oxford: Oxford University Press, 1981.

Miller, Marv. *Suicide After Sixty: The Final Alternative.* New York: Springer Publishing Co., 1979.

Osgood, Nancy J. *Suicide in the Elderly.* Rockville, Md.: Aspen Publishers, 1985.

Padovano, Anthony. *Free to Be Faithful.* New York: Paulist Press, Educational Services, 1972.

Parker, A. Morgan, Jr. *Suicide Among Young Adults.* New York: Exposition Press, 1974.

Pearson, Linnea, with Ruth Purtilo. *Separate Paths: Why People End Their Lives.* San Francisco: Harper & Row, 1977.

Peck, Michael L., Norman L. Farberow, and Robert E. Litman. *Youth Suicide.* New York: Springer Publishing Co., 1985.

Perlin, Seymour, ed. *A Handbook for the Study of Suicide.* New York: Oxford University Press, 1975.

Pfeffer, Cynthia R. *The Suicidal Child.* New York: Guilford Press, 1986.

Phipps, William E. "Christian Perspectives on Suicide," *The Christian Century,* Oct. 30, 1985, 970–973.

———. *Death: Confronting the Reality.* Atlanta: John Knox Press, 1987.

Pope, Whitney. *Durkheim's Suicide: A Classic Analyzed.* Chicago: University of Chicago Press, 1976.

Portwood, Doris. *Commonsense Suicide: The Final Right.* Los Angeles and New York: Hemlock Society, 1983.

Pretzel, Paul W. *Understanding and Counseling the Suicidal Person.* Nashville: Abingdon Press, 1972.

Quinnett, Paul G. *Suicide: The Forever Decision.* New York: Continuum Publishing Co., 1987.

Rabkin, Brenda. *Growing Up Dead.* Nashville: Abingdon Press, 1978.

Richman, Joseph. *Family Therapy and Suicidal People.* New York: Springer Publishing Co., 1985.

Rollin, Betty. *Last Wish.* New York: Linden Press/Simon & Schuster, 1985.

Rosenfeld, Linda, and Marilynne Prupas. *Left Alive: After a Suicide Death in the Family.* Springfield, Ill.: Charles C Thomas, 1984.

Shneidman, Edwin. *Definition of Suicide.* New York: John Wiley & Sons, 1985.

———. *Voices of Death.* New York: Harper & Row, 1980.

Shneidman, Edwin S., and Norman L. Farberow, eds. *Clues to Suicide.* New York: McGraw-Hill Book Co., 1957.

Stengel, Erwin. *Suicide and Attempted Suicide.* Baltimore: Penguin Books, 1964.

Stone, Howard W. *Suicide and Grief.* Philadelphia: Fortress Press, 1972.

Szasz, Thomas S. "The Ethics of Suicide," *Antioch Review* 31 (Spring 1971), 7–17.

United Methodist Church. *Book of Resolutions 1988.* Nashville: Abingdon Press, 1988. See the resolution on suicide.

U.S. Department of Health and Human Services. Public Health Service. *Monthly Vital Statistics Report.* Washington, D.C.: Government Printing Office.

Varah, Edward Charles, ed. *The Samaritans: To Help Those Tempted to Suicide or Despair.* New York: Macmillan Co., 1966.

Wallace, M. A. "The Nurse in Suicide Prevention," *Nursing Outlook* 15, no. 3 (March 1967), 55–57.

Wekstein, Louis. *Handbook of Suicidology: Principles, Problems, and Practice.* New York: Brunner/Mazel, 1979.

Wesley, John. "Thoughts on Suicide." *The Works of John Wesley,* 3rd ed., vol. 13, 481. Grand Rapids: Baker Book House, 1979.

Wiesel, Elie. "Jonah," in *Five Biblical Portraits,* 129–155. Notre Dame, Ind.: University of Notre Dame Press, 1981.

Zusman, J., and D. L. Davidson, eds. *Organizing the Community to Prevent Suicide.* Springfield, Ill.: Charles C Thomas, 1971.

## Journals Focusing on Suicide

*The Bulletin of Suicidology.*

*Hemlock Quarterly.* Published by the Hemlock Society.

*Omega: An International Journal for the Study of Dying, Death, Bereavement, Suicide and Other Lethal Behaviors.*

*Suicide and Life Threatening Behavior.* Official publication of the American Association of Suicidology. Previous titles: *Life Threatening Behavior,* vols. 1–4 for 1971–1974, and *Suicide,* vol. 5 for 1975.

*The Youth Suicide Prevention NETwork News.* Published by the Human Services Development Institute, Center for Research and Advanced Study, University of Southern Maine.

## Movies, Plays, and Television Resources

*ABC Notebook: Teen Suicide.* A documentary by the American Broadcasting Company. Available on videotape.

*A Better Way: Addressing the Issue of Suicide.* A 1988 production by Multimedia Ministries International (with Pastoral Counseling for Denver).

*Filmmakers Library.* Annual catalogs available from 133 East 58th Street, New York, NY 10022.

*It Doesn't Have to End This Way.* A thirty-minute video. Available from the Arkansas Youth Suicide Prevention Commission, 301 State Capitol, Little Rock, AR 72201.

*'Night, Mother.* A play by Marsha Norman. New York: Hill & Wang, 1983. Won the 1983 Pulitzer Prize for Drama; later a film.

*Permanent Record.* Paramount Pictures, 1988. Written by Jarre Fees, Alice Liddle, and Larry Ketron.

*Right of Way.* A film by George Schaefer. Reviewed by Gerald E. Forshey, "Film Criticism in a Christian Perspective," *The Christian Century,* Nov. 9, 1983, 1007–1008.

*Right to Die.* A television drama written by Phil Penningroth for the National Broadcasting Company.

*Silence of the Heart.* A television drama written by Phil Penningroth.

*Whose Life Is It, Anyway?* A play by Brian Clark. New York: Dodd, Mead, 1978. Later produced as a film. Subject of a "Personal Perspective" by Gloria Maxson in *The Christian Century,* Oct. 20, 1982, 1038–1040.

*Young People in Crisis.* A thirty-minute video featuring Dr. Pamela Cantor, Chair, National Committee on Youth Suicide Prevention. Available from EXAR Communications, Inc., 267 B McClean Avenue, Staten Island, NY 10305. Especially helpful for parents, teachers, and other workers with youth.

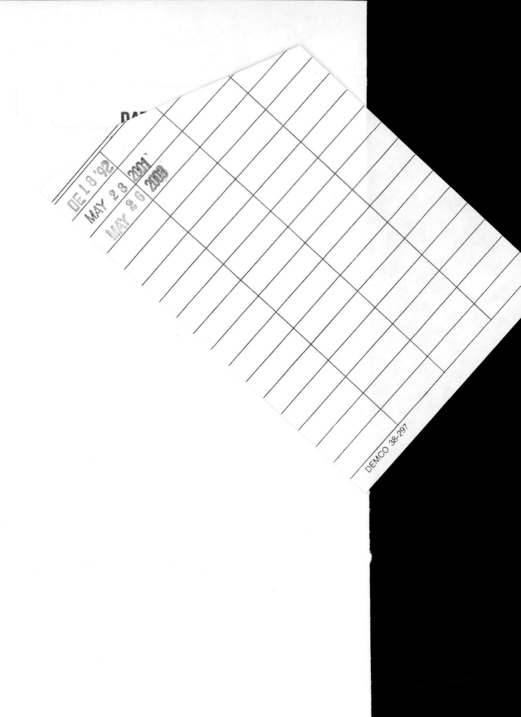